PIONEER PREACHERS IN PARADISE

The Legacies of George Liele, Prince Williams and Thomas Paul In Jamaica, the Bahamas and Haiti

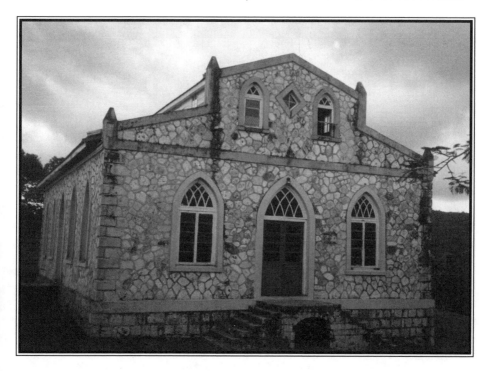

ALFRED LANE PUGH

Front Cover photo: Watford Baptist Church, Hopewell, Jamaica
(Hanover Parish)

Copyright © 2003 Alfred Lane Pugh

ISBN: 1-59196-293-5

All rights reserved.

Prepared by North Star Press of St. Cloud, Inc., St. Cloud,
Minnesota 56302

Printed by Versa Press, Inc., East Peoria, Illinois

Published by:
Paradise Publishing

CONTENTS

Prologue

Introduction

Dedication and Acknowledgments

PART I
Baptist Origins and Development in Jamaica

1	George Liele: Pioneer Ordained Black Missionary
2	Jamaica Before Liele
3	George Liele in Jamaica: Baptist Pioneer
4	Moses Baker: Liele's Colleague in Evangelism
5	Native Baptist: Spirit Christians
6	The British Missionary Society
7	The Legacy of George Liele: Non-Violent Activism
8	The Liele Legacy: Free Education
9	The Liele Legacy: Jamaica Baptist Missions
10	The Liele Legacy: Baptist Fruit of Emancipation
11	The Liele Legacy: Afro-Jamaican Baptist Leadership
12	What Church Denomination Speaks for The Masses?

PART II
Baptists in the Bahama Islands

13	Pioneer Black Preachers in The Bahamas
14	The Bahama Islands Before Prince Williams
15	Prince Williams Honored as Pioneer Baptist Church Founder

16	The British Missionary Presence in the Bahamas
17	Daniel Wilshere: British Missionary/Venerated Bahamian Churchman
18	The Legacy of Prince Williams and Other Baptists

PART III
Baptist Origins and Development in Haiti

19	Thomas Paul: African-American Baptist Missionary
20	Haiti Before Thomas Paul: 1492-1832
21	The Slave's Religion: A Contributing Factor for Revolt
22	Baptist Missions in Haiti
23	Missionaries From England and Jamaica
24	Haitian Baptist Pioneers and Church Builders
25	Haitian Mission Efforts by Baptists From the United States
26	Why Baptists and Other Protestants Have Not Impacted Haiti (as in Jamaica and the Bahama Islands)
27	Unpredictable Signs of Hope

PROLOGUE

Three personal events which occurred over a span of several years contributed to the research, writing, and publication of this book. The first was the result of doing the research necessary to complete a thesis assignment required for graduation from Lincoln University Theological Seminary in Pennsylvania. My thesis subject was "A Historical Study of the Ministry and Laity in Negro Baptist Churches." The only book about my intended subject in the seminary library was *The History of The Negro Church* by Carter G. Woodson. I was introduced to George Liele (a.k.a. George Lisle) the founder and organizer of the first African Baptist churches in Savannah, Georgia, and Kingston, Jamaica. In fact, I had never read anything about the history of the black religious experience in the United States.

In 1989, a member of the church of which I was Senior Pastor in Fort Lauderdale, Florida, gave me a copy of a handbook, entitled, *The Gleaner, Geography and History of Jamaica* that, since Independence Day 1962, has been required reading for every child attending primary and secondary school in Jamaica. Although three of the seven national heroes of Jamaica are pictured, praised and presented on the book cover as Baptist clergy. However, the book inaccurately (perhaps factitiously) credits the beginning of Baptist Churches presence in Jamaica to the arrival of English clergy of the British Missionary Society in 1814. For more than forty years, the children of Jamaica have been denied the opportunity to read the glorious story of and fully appreciate the memory of George Liele and Moses Baker, internationally known and honored African-American Baptist pioneers who literally placed the Bible in Afro-Jamaican hands.

The second event that contributed to the writing of this book was a renewed interest in George Liele that came in 1997 when I read Clement Gayle's book, *George Liele, Pioneer Missionary to Jamaica*. I spent the next five years uncovering additional historical data from primary and secondary sources and enlarging my research to include the lives and contributions of Liele and other pioneer Baptist preachers who were the "fathers" of the Baptist witness in the Bahama Islands and Haiti.

The third event is the way many African Americans and Jamaicans relate to each other. It seems to me that when African Americans speak of Jamaicans, the conversation often focuses on foreign nationality, close-knit family and community traits, or their aggressiveness in pursuing education and property ownership, establishing businesses, and obtaining professional skills. They watch with amazement and some jealousy as Jamaicans organize and develop political organizations and seek and gain public offices. On the other hand, when Jamaicans speak of African Americans, the conversation often attests to their ignorance about the long struggle in which African Americans have engaged to achieve the right to pursue the economic and political goals for which many have come to the United States to enjoy. Even the martyrdom of Dr. Martin Luther King, Jr., is often considered an event of limited significance. Many Jamaicans, as do other people from Caribbean Islands and Africa, resist being labeled African American or black. They prefer citizen classification on the basis of national origin.

Perhaps, at some time in the future, the descendants of the African Diaspora will realize that in this world where European and Western culture reigns supreme, our international origin continues to provide the basis of our minority citizenship—a factor that supercedes nationality. To that end, this writer hopes that the thesis of this book will be declared and debated from pulpits and lecture halls, in churches and classrooms. There is an historic religious-cultural gospel thread that connects the African people of the United States, Jamaica, the Bahamas and Haiti that began more than two hundred years ago when black preachers founded the first independent Baptist churches and emigrated from British North America to introduce new freedoms that contributed to our development. In a word, all of us, no matter the denomination we claim, are the recipients of a Baptist heritage. Our commonalities must be admitted, learned, appreciated, and used to marshal us as a diaspora people to achieve our rightful destiny. Our history, so often unknown, denied or forgotten must be rescued from obscurity.

INTRODUCTION

This book is about former slaves from the British North American colonies of Georgia and New York (via Spanish East Florida) who, as free men, founded Baptist Churches and established religious, educational, political, and economic legacies which form the foundation of the island nations of Jamaica and the Bahama Islands. Because of their pioneering efforts and an abbreviated mission evaluation effort by a Baptist preacher from Boston, Massachusetts, an invisible but undeniably religious-cultural gospel thread of Christianity was initiated that has, for more than two centuries, connected the descendants of African people living in the United States with the descendants of African people of Jamaica, the Bahama Islands, Haiti, and other islands of the Greater Caribbean Basin.

The African American Baptist preachers who became the founders of the African Baptist church movement as the Revolutionary War was coming to an end, for the most part, are unknown, forgotten or ignored, by Baptists and others in North America. Only recently have efforts been made to rectify that sobering oversight.

Part I and Part II of this book introduce and discuss the missions and legacies of the African American Baptist preachers who were among the first to preach the Christian Gospel to the slave and free black populations of the islands of Jamaica and the Bahamas. They struggled against formidable odds to overcome cultural barriers, racial and religious persecution, physical punishment, and imprisonment. With few material resources but with vision and determination, they persevered when, in the words of the poet, James Weldon Johnson, "faith unborn had died."[1]

The study of pioneer black preachers and church founders and their movements did not occur in a socio-historic vacuum. It would be incomplete and inadequate apart from the contextual history of each island that includes how African slavery began and the development of the religion of the slaves and freedmen before and after exposure to Christianity by African-Americans and Europeans. These are not separated or isolated foci but are interwoven into the history of each nation. Building on the pioneering efforts of George Liele, Prince Williams, and other Baptist preachers (Native Baptist and European missionaries), social, economic and political activities began in Jamaica and the Bahamas that set in place the foundations of free education for poor and downtrodden enslaved Africans and manumitted blacks. Simultaneously, as once enslaved people gained religious liberty and began to strive for the opportunity to participate in representative government and develop entrepreneurial enterprise and become property owners, they found leadership and support from Baptist church leaders.

Part III presents the story of the Baptist presence in Haiti, an island country which is certainly one of the most unique in the Caribbean Basin. It was within a national historic context that the Afro-Baptist Church movement was born and developed in Jamaica and the Bahamas. However, as we juxtapose the history of those islands with the historical development of Haiti, we are able to discern and understand the failure of the Afro-Baptist church movement to develop significantly enough to exert influence to modify and shape the institutions of that island. Afro-Baptist ministers and churches were never able to influence the events that prevented the development of participatory democracy for the Haitian people nor did they contribute to a nationwide system of free education for all or freedom for all from fear and government initiated violence. This book proposes several reasons why the people of Haiti have not been strongly and positively impacted by Protestant Christianity in general and the preaching and teaching effort of African-American Baptists in particular. The enduring poverty, except for the privileged one percent, among the people of Haiti, the lack of opportunity, and the inability of national leadership to establish enduring democratic government in tandem with supporting social institutions and traditions, are also lifted up for examination and discussion.

Finally, in this book, the reader will confront two contemporary concerns. The first is the postulation that there is no Christian denomination, religious, social or political group operating with a religious setting that speaks or advocates for the Jamaican and Haitian masses as the Afro- and Native Baptists did in the nineteenth and the first half of the twentieth century. On the other hand, the Baptist presence in the Bahamas continues to represent effectively the aspirations of the majority population and is the nation's largest denomination numerically speaking.

The second contemporary concern is the overwhelming evidence indicating that Neo-African religions such as Convince and Cumina in Jamaica and Vodun (or Voodoo) in Haiti remain pervasive forces, especially among the illiterate and impoverished city masses and rural poor. These Neo-African religions and elements of North American Pentecostal Christianity, seem to contribute to national divisions that prohibit unity, progress, stability, and peace.

Note

[1] James Weldon Johnson, "Lift Every Voice and Sing," *The National Baptist Hymnal* (Nashville, National Baptist Publishing Board, 1977), p 477.

DEDICATION AND ACKNOWLEDGMENTS

This book is dedicated to my father. Wilfred Benjamin Pugh emigrated to the United States from his home in the village of Hopewell in Hanover Parish of northwestern Jamaica to attend Virginia Union College and Seminary in Richmond. His ambition was to follow in the footsteps of the parson of the Watford Baptist Church of which the Pugh family had been faithful members for many years. The land for the church cemetery located across the street from the church, which I have seen, was the gift of the Pugh family. For many of our childhood years, my father held my sister, brother, and me spellbound as he spoke about preaching as a boy on the sea shore. His pulpit, he told us many times, was a certain tree stump; his congregation— always the crashing waves and waving palm trees.

He often proudly spoke of his involvement in the Marcus Garvey movement known as the Universal Negro Improvement Association (UNIA). An avid reader and "race man," he would have appreciated the story of the contributions of former African-American slaves who became the founders of the Baptist witness in the island colony and nation of his birth; the black men who contributed to the development of the freedoms the Jamaican people have enjoyed.

Many other people influenced and supported me in completing this work. Foremost among those is my beloved wife, Cleora. In spite of the financial burden the years of my research, study, and travel placed on our family, she has always been an endless fountain of enthusiasm for all of my endeavors in ministry, as an educator, historian, and aspiring writer. I could not have mastered our computer to complete this manuscript without her patient instruction.

I am greatly indebted to the Reverend Michael C. Symonette whose research on George Liele resulted in the book that inspired this initial writing effort. References to Symonette's book appear frequently throughout this work. Dr. David T. Shannon, the former president of Virginia Union University and Andover Theological Seminary, a friend and colleague of three decades, has been my "sounding board" for clarifying ideas and theories in many research areas. He has never hesitated to volunteer helpful suggestions and constructive criticism.

My friend and colleague, the Reverend John Roker, enthusiastically provided invaluable assistance and resources that augmented my research. His knowledge about the Bahamas and Bahamian Baptist church history was critically helpful as was his ability to arrange interviews with the Reverend Michael C. Symonette and other brethren of the Bahamas Baptist Union. Finally, a friend and fellow Lincoln University alumnus, Thomas D. Williams, graciously, but critically reviewed my manuscript and provided professional grammatical advice and suggestions to drastically improve it.

The research and writing of this book has taken more than five years to complete and many individuals, in addition to those mentioned, directly or indirectly assisted in its conception and publication. To all, I owe so much for their questions, comments, suggestions, and encouragement.

Alfred Lane Pugh
Lauderhill, Florida

PART I
Baptist Origins and Development in Jamaica

Chapter One

GEORAGE LIELE: PIONEER ORDAINED BLACK MISSIONARY

Liele's Early Years in Colonial Georgia

There is an invisible but undeniable religious-cultural gospel thread of Christianity that has for more than two centuries connected the descendants of African people living in the United States with the descendants of African people of Jamaica, the Bahama Islands, Haiti, and the Greater Caribbean Basin. That thread began with a slave preacher whose name was George Liele. Liele (a.k.a. Lisle) was born about 1750 or 1751 in the English colony of Virginia. His parents, remembered only by their first names, Liele and Nancy, were slaves of Henry (a.k.a.Harry) Sharpe. Early in life, Liele and his parents were taken to Kiokee in Burke Country (now Columbia County), New Georgia. Most of the men living in New Georgia (the name was shortened after the Revolutionary War) in the early years had been felons in English prisons, released on condition that they relocate to populate the Georgia colony in North America. The eminent historian, John Hope Franklin wrote, "Georgia is unique among the English colonies in three of the restrictions the colonial trustees placed on the settlers. There were to be no free land titles, no alcoholic beverages, and no Negro slaves. . . . The trustees were determined to keep slavery out. They reasoned that the colonists would be too poor to purchase slaves, and it would be demoralizing if some had slaves and some did not."[1]

This policy changed when the prohibition of blacks as slaves was overcome in 1750 because of the continuous pressure of slave holders from nearby South Carolina. By the time Henry

Sharpe and his family and slaves arrived, there was a population of about 23,000 in the colony including 15,000 slaves. In 1753, the colonists adopted a slave code. One of the stringent restraints on slave life was that they were not to be taught to read or write. Slave owner Henry Sharpe disobeyed the law and permitted some of his slaves, including George Liele, to learn to read and write. Liele's communication skills have been documented by the many letters he wrote dating from 1790 to 1802 to the Reverend John Rippon, one of the founders of the British Mission Society and the publisher of its newsletter, *The Baptist Annual Register*, in which Liele's letters appeared.[2]

Baptist Christianity on the Sharpe Plantation

Henry Sharpe and other owners of slaves observed Sunday as if it were the Hebrew (Jewish) Sabbath, a day of rest for man and beast. He encouraged, or perhaps required, his slaves to accompany him to plantation services at the Buckhead Creek Baptist Church. Worship was required even though slaves were assigned special seats apart from whites. Segregated seating in Christian churches was one of the early forms of segregation in southern and northern colonial America. Nevertheless, George Liele and his family were regarded as an integral part of slave owner Sharpe's church fellowship. Some church historians refer to those worship experiences to substantiate a conditioning, they believe, the deferential and patronizing attitude Liele exhibited towards Caucasians.[3] Other writers, however, argue that there is no reason to doubt that an enterprising slave would not have used his early exposure and experiences around his slave masters to study carefully their habits and develop certain personal relational techniques which would be beneficial later in the achievement of his goals and objectives. Later events seem to indicate that Liele mastered the art of effectively maximizing the benevolent good will of slave-owning whites like Henry Sharpe while maximizing the limitations of his condition.

There may have been several reasons why Henry Sharpe was willing to teach his slaves to read and write, treating them humanely even though he knew that colonial punishment for such deeds could be severe. For one thing, it is generally acknowledged that he was a deacon in the Buckhead Creek Baptist Church. His spiritual sensitivity was probably the result of his association with his pastor, the Reverend Matthew Moore who, in turn, may have been influenced by two English preachers, George Whitfield and John Wesley. The "hell and damnation" emotion that filled sermons of those two powerful and persuasive preachers was the major cause of the Evangelical Revival known as the Great Awakening in England and the English colonies of North America that lasted more than thirty years, from 1739 to 1770. The Great Awakening is believed to have been the greatest spiritual event ever witnessed in America. "Old congregations, such as Methodists and Baptists, attracted new worshipers. These God-fearing and dissenting people challenged the old order. Baptists became anathema to members of the plantocracy whose very culture was deemed sinful by these new religious groups. Baptists defended individual and minority group interests . . . and could be dubbed subversive of tradition, ranging from aspects of religion through politics and economics."[4]

The pastor of the Sharpe plantation church, Reverend Matthew Moore, stressed the evangelical emphasis of personal conversion, salvation and the importance of each individual's acceptance of Jesus Christ as Savior and Lord before baptism and church membership. Slaves and whites desiring baptism had to stand before their respective congregations and testify or provide evidence that their motives were sincere. George Liele, in a letter to John Rippon, reflects the biblical hermeneutics of Matthew Moore when he wrote that when he was converted he made intercession with Jesus Christ "for the salvation of my poor immortal soul, and . . . requested of my Lord and Master to give me a work . . ."[5] There is no reason to doubt that at the moment of conversion, Liele's understanding of the word "master" was changed forever. While a man named Sharpe "owned" his body, Jesus Christ was his "Master." He may have never overtly stated that in a sermon, but he did not hesitate sharing his testimony with Rippon.

Undoubtedly, Henry Sharpe's concern for his slaves' spiritual development was unusual compared to most slave owners. From early colonial years until about 1730, with one or two exceptions (especially the Quakers), religious denominations and slave owners were not encouraged to expose slaves to Christianity. Therefore, many slaves developed their own religious rituals and services based primarily on the religious traditions of their African tribal heritage. Frequently, however, as Eugene O. Genovese' observations are summarized, they incorporated religious experiences they observed in colonial America. One such ritual involved something similar to the Christian baptism service and was usually held near a river or creek. Also, many elderly slaves living along the eastern Carolina costal regions were Muslims from West Africa. They continued their practice of burying the dead so that their faces were directed toward the sunrise. Other African burial customs and practices became a part of local burial practices and continued for many decades even by those who adopted Christianity later on. Grave markings in slave burial grounds in Georgia were found to be similar to grave markings in West Africa. The fact that slave funeral services were held at night was indicative of the strong influence of African tribal religious traditions.[6]

Most of the time and energy of early colonial white ministers, especially in the south, was spent upon the planters and their families. They neglected the slave population because they did not want to be faced with the embarrassing possibility of creating a situation which might result in slave manumission or revolts. There was also uncertainty about whether slaves who accepted Christianity could be held in bondage by other Christians. However, political pressure applied by slave traders in Liverpool assured English planters in America and the Sugar Islands of the West Indies that freedom in Jesus Christ did not extend to civil rights. Until the Great Awakening crusades of the 1700s, the Quakers being the exception, it was understood that the body of a slave could be chained even when his soul was free of sins.

Liele's Conversion and Call

In 1773, just a few years before the Revolutionary War began, George Liele, by then twenty-three or twenty-four years of age, and several other slaves were converted and then baptized by the Reverend Moore at the church on the Sharpe plantation. About that event, Liele, writing to John Ripon in December 1791 and published in the *Baptist Annual Register*, wrote that "at the moment of his conversion he accepted Jesus Christ as his Lord and Master . . . he considered his baptism service a Christian rite-of-passage event, "a turning point of his life."[7] In that same letter, he also expressed great appreciation for the contributions towards his personal development by the Reverend Moore and other white Christian ministers and teachers.

The Baptist historian, Lewis Jordan, substantiates Barnes' contention that, before the Civil War, most of the white Christians were Baptists and Methodist from the north who traveled to the south just to preach to slaves and poor whites. They were, he wrote, the significant reason "that early Black preachers became versed in Bible study, theological simplicities and elements of Christian doctrine and faith. The educational opportunities and speaking experiences the slave preachers gained from the white preachers and teachers helped establish Black preachers, such as George Liele and others who followed him, as prominent slave and free Black community leaders, the first of their racial group to be exposed to western knowledge."[8]

Liele, who was sometimes called "Brother George" by friends, quickly demonstrated a convincing gift for preaching to fellow slaves on the Sharpe plantation. He endeavored to instruct them in Biblical knowledge and Christian hymns. Years later he would say that his method of teaching and preaching was crude but firm and unyielding in sense and purpose. The Reverend Moore helped Liele improve his communication skills. Impressed with Liele's ability and passion for preaching, he arranged a trial sermon before a group of preachers at a quarterly meeting of the local Baptist Ministers Association. The association licensed Liele to preach, probably with the understanding that a white person would be present. He was prohibited from baptizing anyone or performing weddings. The action of the all-white Baptist association seems to affirm the fact that there was no attempt on the part of most Evangelical Christian clergy to introduce a special, or lesser, method for qualifying blacks to preach. In Liele's situation, his owner, Henry Sharpe not only approved of his "call" and licensing but arranged to have him preach every month to the entire plantation, black and white.[9]

Undoubtedly, a slave owner like Sharpe must have known that many, if not most slave owners were callous and conscienceless, regarding their slaves as cheap labor for their profit making enterprises. In fact, for some, if they valued religion for their slave population at all, Christianity was another mechanism used for teaching them to be obedient and docile. Many Southern churchmen preached to slaves only to defend the institution of slavery, upholding their condition with scriptural authority. Their Biblical references and sermons were chosen to endorse and promote the scheme of bondage and the doctrine of contentment and humility.

But there were also other white church folk, like Sharpe, as Mason Crum contends, whose "desire to evangelize the slaves was prompted not only by the normal enthusiasm of the Christian church to uplift a lowly people, but by a deep, though unexpressed, sense that there was something inherently wrong about slavery. Their enthusiasm for slave conversions was at least a compensation for a felt wrong. Many good men and women became involved in a situation from which they could not extricate themselves. Christianization of the slaves became in part a form of release."[10] Some may have chosen to live in poverty so that they would be able to evangelize slaves whenever and wherever they could. They probably considered it their solemn duty. Undoubtedly, they believed that what they were doing proved the genuineness of their profession.

Whether those who presented the Bible to the slaves meant to use its teachings for evil or good, the fact remains that there were several benefits from that exposure that had long-term benefits and consequences for the race as a whole in the British

North American and Caribbean colonies. First, when slave owners permitted their slaves to hear the Bible read or taught them to read it, opportunities were provided for the slaves to create a communal basis for communication—a common language. Never to be forgotten is the fact that when they were captured or sold into slavery, they were members of various tribes or families, each with a different language or dialect. Also, for the most part, each tribe worshiped a different deity. When shipped to colonial America, a major, and for the most part, successful effort was made by those who enslaved them to destroy their tribal and family continuity. That "uprooting" process was just one of many attempts to destroy everything the slaves may have had in common other than color. However, by overtly adapting to Christianity, they also were adapting it to themselves. The language of the Bible, as they heard it, was utilized to mitigate an existential need and situation. It became their way of establishing a system of communication (language) for conversation and communal singing. In the most elementary sense, the words, language and sounds of the Bible became a practical means of developing verbal communication among the slaves that was also acceptable to those who enslaved them. Interestingly, while the slave owners strictly forbade drumming, they encouraged and appreciated slave singing. Singing slaves, they concluded, was evidence of happy slaves.

Second, those slaves who became the preachers became their community's first leaders, no matter whether they were approved by the whites (like George Liele) or self-appointed and promoted as were slave revolt leaders such as Gabriel Prosser and Nat Turner. A third consequence of being exposed to the Bible, was the development of the slaves and freedmen's first local and national organizations and institutions, the invisible and the institutional Black church.

Liele: Preacher, Evangelist and Church Founder

With the permission of his owner, George Liele, in 1775, was ordained to the Christian Ministry by the same ministers who had previously licensed him to preach—the Baptist Association of

1773 English map showing southern South Carolina border along Savannah River showing Galphins Mill and Silver Bluff.

Burke County. He was given permission by Henry Sharpe to travel up and down the Savannah River. For four years he preached to other slaves (and whites) on surrounding plantations, wherever other slave owners permitted, in Burke County, Yamacraw (a suburb of Savannah) Brumpton, and Savannah in the Georgia

First African Baptist Church, Savannah.

colony. Liele was also granted permission to preach on the Province of South Carolina side of the river at a plantation in Orangeburg Precinct (just south and east of New Windsor Township) at Galphins Mill. The area today is located about twelve miles from Augusta, in Aiken County.[11] The area known as Galphinton and Fort Galphin was owned by a liberal and humane Irishman named George Galphin.

David George, a black man living with the Indians after escaping from a plantation in Essex County, Virginia, was engaged in trading deer skins with Mr. Galphin in the area on the Savannah River George knew as Silver Bluff. On one of his trading visits, George asked, and Galphin agreed, to let him live at Silver Bluff as his personal servant. Many years later, as a Baptist minister in Sierra Leone, West Africa, David George wrote a letter to John Rippon of London that was published in the *Baptist Register*. He reported that he had heard George Liele preach and was deeply impressed. This was probably at the church at Silver Bluff, for the Galphin family and other whites. Slaves were permitted to attend but were seated in a section reserved for them. Some time afterwards, George, was baptized by a man he called Brother Palmer.[12] A missionary from Stonington, Connecticut, the Reverend Palmer, organized George and several other slaves into a church and gave them the Lord's Supper somewhere in the Silver Bluff area. Under Liele's guidance, George, who taught himself to read, began to preach. With Mr. Galphin's approval, Palmer, assisted by George Liele, organized a plantation church for slave worship.[13] Its first pastor was the Reverend Palmer. Liele also preached for the slave congregation with whites present as required by colonial law.

An historical document printed for the Bicentennial Celebration of Augusta, Georgia in 1935, states parenthetically, that there was a 'Dead River Church' organized in 1750, near Silver Bluff Landing on the Carolina side of the Savannah River, originally built for whites but (was) turned over to the Negroes in 1773."[14] If this revelation is accurate, it raises the possibility that when the slaves took over the building, they called it the Silver Bluff Church.

Later, David George, in his own words, "began to exhort in the church, and learned to sing hymns." He was appointed to the office of Elder and was instructed on his duties and responsibilities by Brother Palmer. He continued preaching at Silver Bluff, the group increased "eight to thirty or more, . . . till the British came to the city of Savannah and took it."[15] George, his family, and many of the Silver Bluff members left the Silver Bluff area and settled, first at Ebenezer, about twenty miles from Savannah and then closer to the British military near Savannah. Shortly afterwards, he and his family were among the first group of slaves and about five hundred whites who, in 1782, left Georgia for the British colony of Nova Scotia. As a freeman and an ordained minister, he was granted permission by Governor Parr of Nova Scotia to continue his ministry. In 1784 he organized a church in Shelburn (Nova Scotia) composed of a mixed racial congregation of sixty members. Ten years later, to escape the cold winter weather, George was among the 12,000 people of color who left Nova Scotia to settle in Sierra Leone, West Africa.[16]

A second slave influenced by George Liele became a preacher and church organizer in New Providence, Bahama Islands. According to Liele, Brother Amos (as he was known) was a member of either the church at Silver Bluff (South Carolina) or Savannah (Georgia). "Reverend Amos," as he was also known, is believed to have convinced his members in Nassau to construct a church house.[17] The absence of any known documentation and his years of ministry suggests that the congregation did not continue in existence. However, the Reverend Amos may well have been the Amos Williams who is recorded as having sold Prince Williams the land on which Bethel Baptist Church was built. This probability will be discussed in more detail in an ensuing chapter.

The Impact of the Revolutionary War (1776-1783)

Soon after Liele was ordained, the people of Georgia were caught up in the rising tide of political and social discontent and the quest for independence by some which climaxed in the

Revolutionary War of 1776. The war continued for seven years until 1783. Plantation slave owners and others who chose to remain supportive of the King of England and wanted Georgia to remain an English colony were called Loyalists. However, because of the constant harassment and physical violence inflicted on them by the Patriots, colonists who wanted immediate independence from England, the Loyalists were forced to seek refuge under the protection of the English military at a fort on Tybee Island. Many slaves discovered that they too, for the first time, had an opportunity to choose which side deserved their loyalty. The English military occupying Savannah announced that all slaves who joined them would gain their freedom when the colonial revolt was crushed. It was obvious to the slaves that the English military was far superior to the rag-tail group of men who called themselves Patriots. Therefore, they had two reasons for abandoning the plantations and slipping away to join the British and their Loyalists supporters on fortified Tybee Island, located about twenty miles east of Savannah, where the Savannah River empties into the Atlantic Ocean. Other slaves who did not choose to seek the protection of the English or their promise of freedom after the revolt, simply moved to Savannah or Augusta.

When Liele's benevolent owner, Harry Sharpe, joined the British Army as a commissioned officer, Liele and his family went with him. Liele not only attached himself to the English forces but began to hold Christian worship services, eventually organizing the slaves and free blacks into a Tybee Island church. That was easily accomplished because many of the blacks on the island had already heard about Liele and some had been under his influence previously. During this period, George Liele frequently traveled to Savannah to organize the independent congregation of that city in 1777. It was called "First African Baptist Church" of Savannah and was composed of members from the Silver Bluff Church and Liele's Tybee Island church and other former slaves and free blacks from Savannah city and environs.

Liele found that George Bryan, another slave converted under his preaching and baptized by him, was among the slaves from the Silver Bluff Church who had also sought refuge with the English military in Savannah. Liele and ministers of the white

Baptist Association ordained Bryan and were very influential in helping him organize the former Silver Bluff slaves and others into what is known as the "First Bryan Baptist Church" of Savannah. The organization of both churches, First African and First Bryan, and the ordination and ministries of the Reverend George Liele up and down the Savannah River area unequivocally attest to the unusual respect the white Baptist brethren held for him.

Today, visitors are invited to view the minutes and records of both churches which also list the names of the founding members who were baptized by George Liele as members of either the church at Silver Bluff, South Carolina or on Tybee Island, Georgia. Original eighteenth century written (by slaves) church minutes as well as the letters from the white Baptist Association authenticating their historic viability are also on display in both churches. The churches, always independently controlled by African-Americans, are located less than two blocks apart in the old historic section of Savannah.[18]

Slaves, members of what became the Silver Bluff Church congregation, who did not join Liele on the Tybee Island or Liele or George in Savannah, moved to Augusta, Georgia. In 1891, led by Jesse Peters, they formed the Springfield Baptist Church.[19]

Harry Sharpe, Liele's benefactor, died on Tybee Island while serving as an officer in the English military, but not before he granted Liele his freedom. That act of manumission was quickly contested by Sharpe's family. Liele was jailed pending a review of his case by a military court. Fortunately, a British officer known only as Colonel Kirkland, was instrumental in securing Liele's release, providing papers that verified his free status.[20] That narrow escape from being returned to the status of slave hastened Liele's efforts to join other free blacks and run-away-slaves fleeing colonial Georgia and other colonies for the opportunity to live in a British colony, either Nova Scotia, the Bahama Islands or Jamaica. Liele voluntarily indentured himself to Colonel Kirkland by borrowing seven hundred dollars to purchase passage by ship to Jamaica for himself and his family.[21] And so, in December 1782, accompanied by his wife and four children, he boarded a ship in Savannah and sailed to the Caribbean island of Jamaica.

NOTES

[1] John Hope Franklin, *From Slavery to Freedom*, Third Ed. (New York: Alfred A. Knopf, 1967), p. 83.

[2] Clement Gayle, *George Liele, Pioneer Missionary To Jamaica* (Kingston: Jamaica Baptist Union, 1982) p. 10.

[3] Ibid., p. 6, 7.

[4] Ian Barnes, *The Historical Atlas Of The American Revolution* (New York, Rutledge, 2000) pg. 60.

[5] Edward A.. Holmes, printed in *Foundations* (Philadelphia: American Baptist Historical Society, 1966), pp. 353-345.

[6] Eugene O. Genovese, *Roll, Jordan,Roll* (New York, Vantage Books, 1976) pp. 198.

[7] Edward A. Holmes, "*George Liele: Negro Slavery's Prophet of Deliverance,*" The Bapist Quarterly, October 1964, p.333-345.

[8] Lewis G. Jordan, "*The Negro Preacher,*" Baptist, March 1929, pp. 13-14.

[9] Gayle, p. 9.

[10] Mason Crum, *Gullah, Negro Life in the Carolina Sea Islands* (New York: Negro Universities Press, 1968) p. 201.

[11] As shown on a map of the Province of South Carolina by James Cook and published by an Act of Parliament, July 7, 1773.

[12] John Rippon, "Account Of The Life Of Mr. David George", The Baptist Annual Register (1790-1793).

[13] Walter Brooks, "The Priority of the Silver Bluff Church", Journal of Negro History, Vol. VII, No. 32, April 1922, pp. 174-182.

[14] Pageant Book (1735-1935), Augusta Bicentennial, pp. 64-65.

[15] Rippon., p. 476.

[16] Walter H. Brooks, *The Silver Bluff Church* (Washington, D.C.: Press of R. L Pendleton, 1910), pp.16-21.

[17] Ibid., p. 40.

[18] Woodson, pp. 35-38.

[19] Encylopedia of African Religions, 1993 ed. s.v.

[20] Gayle, pp. 8-11; Charles M. Wagner, *Profiles of Black Georgia Baptists* (Atlanta: Bennett Brothers Publishing Co., 1980), p. 32.

[21] Indentured means that Liele signed a contract binding him to work for Kirkland for a given length of time as a servant in Jamaica or until his indebtedness was repaid.

Chapter Two

JAMAICA BEFORE LIELE

How Slavery Began in Jamaica

The native Americans known as Tainos who inhabited the island of Jamaica called it Xayma, which means island of waterfalls, streams and springs. When Christopher Columbus landed on the island in 1493, he called it Yamaye. The Tainos were quickly subdued by the Spanish military allowing settlers to come over from Spanish controlled Hispaniola (now the Dominican Republic and Haiti). The settlers, with the aid of the military, systematically and mercilessly captured as many natives as possible committing them to a life time of severe enslavement on ranches, farms and in mines they hoped would produce gold. Native leaders (chiefs) who resisted the Spaniards were sold off to die working in gold mines in other Spanish controlled colonies.[22]

The Spanish encomienda (colonial slave system) was designed by the Spanish government to give its colonists the legal right to bind the Tainos families to their ranches or farms as property of the government, provided that the natives accepted and "converted" to Roman Catholicism. All Tainos converting to Catholicism were to be rewarded by being baptized and being treated humanely. That did not happen. Instead, conditions for the enslaved natives became so inhumane that Dominican priests attacked the slave system as immoral. Spaniards holding natives under the system, according to the priests, were in danger of mortal sin. One Spanish rancher, Bartholomew de Las Casas, strongly influenced by the Dominican condemnation of slavery, entered the Roman Catholic priesthood. As a priest, Las Casas argued that "the native people were being 'unjustly' enslaved. He petitioned the Spanish King to condone the importation of African slaves, whom he claimed were servile by nature, to replace the dwindling Tainos population. Las Casas encouraged the Roman Catholic Church to endorse the Atlantic Slave Trade and the institutionalizing of African enslavement everywhere. That policy of protecting native Americans from enslavement remained the position of the Church for more than 470 years, until it was repealed in 1965 by the Second Vatican Council.[23] Afterwards, Africans were imported into Jamaica to replace the native Tainos, first as household servants brought from European sources and later, directly from the African continent.

The Enslavement of Africans

More than 747,000 Africans were imported directly from the general area bordering the South Atlantic Ocean (eastern-central Sub-Sahara Africa known as the Windward Coast, Gold Coast, Bight of Benin, Bight of Biafra and Central Africa). In a short period of time, Jamaica became a significant slave destination for ships and an important slave market or depot and storage area for foreign, especially, Spanish, slave supply. Documents indicate that as many as 206,200 slaves were shipped from Jamaica to places where slave labor was scarce and the profits for slaves higher.[24]

In later years, the Spanish government developed a slave system that incorporated slave laws and a belief that the spiritual personality of slaves transcended their slave status. Under that system, slaves who "converted" to Roman Catholic Christianity and were "christened" or baptized, could receive the sacraments and marry with Church approval. Slave owners were required to keep the slave family together.[25]

The Spanish military and all settlers, including Roman Catholic personnel, were forced to withdraw when Jamaica was invaded and conquered by England in 1655. No Catholic Church official returned to the island for 137 years when a priest named Anthony Quigly arrived in 1792 to minister to "the increasing number of (European/White) Catholics from other islands and South America who were settling in Jamaica for commercial purposes."[26]

Even though there were about 150,000 persons of African decent (slaves, freedmen and mulattos) in Jamaica the colonial assembly, composed only of plantation owners or planters, eventually passed and sustained laws to maintain the institution of slavery. Representatives of the Church of England (Anglican) were even less responsive to the condition and needs of the slaves than the Roman Catholics had been. As Simpson points out, "The Church of England in Jamaica in the eighteenth century was the religion of the white settlers and officials; it was not a missionary church for the slaves."[27] Simpson also argues that although the Anglican Church in 1701, by a royal charter of the King of England, had organized the Society for the Propagation of the Gospel in Foreign Parts, the Society did not consider the colony of Jamaica as "foreign parts." Anglican priests, therefore, were not instructed to perform religious services to the slave population. They confined their services to white settlers only.[28] Historian Mary Turner is even more pointed when she writes, that the Anglican clergy "often actively engaged in slave management . . . focused on subduing rather than assimilating the Africans . . . ," its missionary efforts "marked by racism and elitism."[29] It seems as if in early eighteenth century Jamaica, God was white.

That color line racism did not improve until missionaries of a German Protestant sect known as Moravians arrived and seriously attempted to evangelize and educate slaves in Biblical knowledge.[30] But in spite of their zealous efforts, their success with the slave population was very limited. The Moravian Church, even to this day, continues to be strongly European in theology and pedantic preaching presentations. Its most serious handicap, however, was it rigidly structured worship services. In short, the slaves did not find Moravian Christianity appealing. Forty-six years of evangelistic effort (1754-1800) resulted in only one thousand slave conversions. Dr. A.G. Waddell, a noted Jamaican scholar, contends that "Religion, like language, is closely identified with the retention of cultural origins."[31]

Pioneer Preachers in Paradise
The Religion of the Slaves

For many years, most Caucasian and a few African-American historians and anthropologists claimed that the terror, horror and suffering that accompanied the systematic destruction of African tribal and family groups during the infamous Middle Passage followed by their disposal at the slave auctions of Europe and the Western Hemisphere, ripped out all substantive memories the slaves may have retained of their culture and religion. However, Melvin Herskovitz, Philip Curtin, Eugene Genovese and other scholars and historians have proven that the people taken from the African continent did not live and exist in a religious vacuum. They were not agnostic, totally devoid of a religious system, without beliefs in the existence of any ultimate reality or anything beyond material phenomena. Genovese, for example, wrote, "the strongest African survivals in Jamaican culture are to be found precisely in religion."[32] Throughout the Caribbean, the focus of African culture was religious. For almost four hundred years, from 1495 to approximately 1880, three major forms of Neo-African or Afro-Caribbean slave religions existed in Jamaica and have continued, in various forms, until the present time. They are known as Obeah, Myalism (also known as Kumina or Cumina) and Convince.

The word, Obeah, is believed to have originated with the Maroons, slaves who escaped from Spanish and British planters and slave owners, and established communities such as Trelawny and Accompong in the mountains of Jamaica. For many years, the British unsuccessfully attempted to recapture or conquer them but were forced, through negotiations, to recognize them as free independent African settlements. Those settlement areas still exist. Most of the people of Accompong were originally from West African tribal groups known as Ashanti, Dahomey and Wyadah. Since Ashanti was the dominant and most numerous tribal groups, the divinities of the Maroons were Ashanti whose protector spirits are called Obia. Thus the Jamaican word, Obeah, came to mean both the "proctor spirit" and the name of a religious social society formed by the slaves for self defense.[33]

Obeah men, considered priests, "worked in secret and concerned themselves largely with private or personal matters such as vendettas. Considered to have been born in West Africa, they used good magic (herbs and folk medications) to heal and bad magic (poison or fear), whatever the situation called for. Their power was based on the Africans' belief in the supernatural which they brought with them from their homeland. The obeah men interpreted the spirit world. The European (English) colonists called their ministrations sorcery. The practice and use of Obeah became a felony punishable by execution, especially when the colonists discovered that the slaves would bind themselves by Obeah oaths in times of slave uprisings and revolt.

Paradoxically, one of the main reasons the planters and slave owners allowed their slaves to be exposed to Christianity was their fear of Obeah.[34] Genovese and Eric Williams (a noted historian and former Prime Minister of Trinidad) spoke and wrote often of the continued strength of the African cults, especially Obeah, not only in Jamaica but in other Caribbean areas (such as the Virgin Islands and the Bahama Islands) even in the twentieth century.[35]

Another Neo-African religion, Myal, or Myalism, differed from Obeah. While Obeah concerned itself primarily with personal or private matters for the members of slave communities in Jamaica, Myalism was basically focused on group worship and welfare. It was initially a male society, similar to West African secret societies. Derived from ancient Ashanti possession tribal religious cults of Dahomy, Myal may have been an older form of Obia that came into existence to challenge Obeah influence. Myalism served as a cover for all religious observances that developed from African religions in Jamaica. Through a ritual dance, the spirit of an ancestor took control (or possessed) the dancer's body, communicating hidden knowledge (through the dancer) to the living. Through the medium of drumming, masks, and other ritual acts, slaves maintained links to their ancestral home.

Myalism provided the slaves two elements, both vital to their survival in a hostile environment. First, the participants gained a sense of belonging, security and hope, in this world and the next, as well as opportunities to gather together to socialize and celebrate. Second, the Myal priests or Myal-men administered mixtures of gunpowder, rum, human blood and grave dirt with oaths and ritual dances. This ceremony provided a feeling of being protected against the demands and abuses (even bullets) of their slave masters. Genovese argues that "Myalism became a . . . politically dangerous tendency . . ." for slave owners. Slaves born into the Ashanti tribal tradition and Myal-men were frequently identified in Caribbean slave revolts. The Myal-men "emerged in enforced hostility to the regime and (helped) curb . . . accommodations attitudes . . ." (Accommodations attitudes define slaves who sought to promote adaptation or compromise towards whites), Obeah and Myal-men seem to have cooperated effectively (with slave leaders) during a number of revolts and disturbances.[36] A form of Myal, known as Kumina and later called Pocamania, became the strongest Neo-African (or Afro-Caribbean) religion in Jamaica.

A third slave religion known as Convince also developed during the years of Christian indifference and benign-neglect, a cult also prominent among the isolated mountain dwelling Maroon people. The leaders of Convince were called, and present day Jamaicans are still called, Bongo Men. While they believed in Obeah not all belonged to Obeah cult groups. They believed in "spirit" but a priest or participant could be "possessed" (when the spirit rode the individual) by more than one spirit (or spirits) at a time. Convince ceremonies were usually held as memorial services in huts. These services also included dancing.[37]

Even though the African influence in the religion of the slaves was basic, it must be emphasized that in no part of the Western Hemisphere where Neo-African religions developed, including Jamaica, were 'religious' Africanisms retained unchanged by the slaves conditions and environment. The slaves from Africa, no matter where they were, developed ways of transforming their African traditions as their lives were impacted by new, and often changing, situations. African styles of worship, forms of ritual, systems of beliefs, and fundamental perspectives were created and have endured on this side of the Atlantic Ocean, not because they were preserved in a "pure" African orthodoxy, but because they were transformed. Especially in British colonies, slaves adapted whatever was useful from the various forms of Christianity or Native American religions as well as their own African religious traditions.

Albert J. Raboteau concurs in this conclusion. He wrote, "Adaptability, based upon respect for spiritual power wherever it originated, accounted for the openness of African religions to syncretize other religious traditions and for continuity of a distinct African religious consciousness."[38] That religious consciousness went unchallenged until the arrival of an indentured black Baptist preacher from the British American colony of Georgia. His universal witness, intuition and organizational gifts set in motion forces that radically altered or modified the religious beliefs and social and cultural conditions of Jamaican slaves and freedmen. He, and those he invited to Jamaica to help him, altered the course of the history of Jamaica forever. His name was George Liele.

Notes

[22] Phillip Sherlock and Hazel Bennett, *The Story of the Jamaican People* (Kingston: Ian Randle Publishers, 1998), pp. 63-67.

[23] Ibid., p. 68.

[24] Philip Curtin, *The Atlantic Slave Trade: A Census* (Madison: University of Wisconsin Press, 1969), pp. 25, 26, 124, 160.

[25] The author has, on two occasions, visited a Roman Catholic church located in Merida, Yucatan (Mexico), constructed for African slaves in 1835 by Spanish cattle ranchers.

[26] George Eaton Simpson, *Black Religion in the New World* (New York: Columbia University Press), 1978, p. 25.

[27] Ibid., p. 27.

[28] Ibid., p. 27.

[29] Mary Turner, *Slaves and Missionaries* (Urbana/Chicago: University of Illinois Press, 1982), p. 66.

[30] The Moravians were a religious group from Germany founded by John Huss in 1722.

[31] D. A.G. Waddell, *The West Indies and the Guianas* (Englewood Cliffs: Prentice-Hall, Inc., 1967), p. 12.

[32] Genovese, p. 173.

[33] Mirian Joel, African Traditions in Latin America (Cuernavaca: Mexico, Centro Intercultural de Documentacion, No. 73, 1977), p. 4-6.

[34] Catherine A. Sunshine, *The Caribbean: Survival, Struggle and Sovereignty* (Washington, D.C.: Ecumenical Program of Central America and the Caribbean, 1973), p.16.

[35] Genovese, p. 172.

[36] Ibid., p. 172, 173.

[37] Joel, p. 4, 9.

[38] Albert J. Raboteau, *Slave Religion* (Oxford: Oxford University Press, 1980), p. 4.

Chapter Three

GEORGE LIELE IN JAMAICA: BAPTIST PIONEER

The Early Years: Entrepreneur and Evangelist

Liele, his wife and four young children, arrived in Jamaica in December 1782.[39] In his possession was a letter of introduction written by his English military patron, Colonel Kirkland. With it, he was able to quickly gain employment with the highest English government official on the island, General Campbell, Governor of Jamaica. Within a period of two years, Liele was able to settle his debt with Colonel Kirkland. He also obtained documents from the Anglican Church vestry (local government) and Governor's office, required under English law, that certified free status for him and his family. When Governor Campbell returned to England in 1785, he gave Liele a letter of recommendation in which he praised him for his high moral character and trustworthiness. In a short time, the industrious Liele was able to support his family by starting and maintaining a thriving freight business.[40]

In spite of his success as an independent businessman, Liele did not forget his commitment to a higher calling: the Christian ministry. He not only became the first black man to preach on the island of Jamaica when he held outdoor evangelistic services at the Kingston Race Course but he was the founder of the Native Baptist Church movement.[41] As in colonial Georgia, many slaves, and some free blacks, were captivated by his persuasive sermons, converted and wanted to be baptized. Liele was unwilling, perhaps prohibited from baptizing anyone while indentured. But when his indentured obligation was satisfied, he applied for a

Certificate of Manumission and was permitted to baptize converts.

In September 1784, Liele began to preach and teach in a private home and subsequently organized a church composed of four baptized converts who were also black immigrants from colonial America. In time, the nucleus became a network of church groups located in many areas, and some beyond the city of Kingston. When the local authorities and officials of the Anglican Church learned of his effort to organize a church for slaves and others, they began to interrupt his services and mentally and physically intimidate him. From that point on, he was periodically persecuted and frequently jailed and chained.[42] The local (white) Presbyterian and Wesleyan Methodists (at first) may have been highly suspicious and critical of Liele's successful and sometimes unorthodox evangelizing efforts, perhaps even suggesting that he was washing feet and "anointing the sick."[43]

Until his movement got underway, the slave and free black population had been generally indifferent to the marginal efforts and appeals of white church representatives. Some of the white clergy may even have been led to believe that the few blacks who had responded to their Euro-centric preaching and worship styles may have regarded being baptized as a protective charm against the "bad" magic of Obeah priests. Therefore, they (the white clergy) were perplexed to see dozens and then hundreds of their slaves and free blacks responding to George Liele—flocking to the seashore near Kingston to be baptized. Liele also conducted immersion baptism services in the river near Spanish Town, located a few miles north of Kingston.

The local authorities were also concerned by the implications of the growing influence Liele seemed to hold over their slaves and the free blacks as well. They were apprehensive even though they knew that Liele only baptized and granted church membership to enslaved blacks who first obtained permission from their owners. The possibility of slave disturbances and rebellion was always uppermost in their minds since the slave population greatly outnumbered them. And so physical and political harassment against Liele intensified even as membership in his groups increased. Even when he preached very orthodox sermons that never overtly encouraged restive disruptive behavior or insurrection and constantly expressed his strong desire that his listeners be freed from sin and its consequences, the pioneer preacher was charged with sedition for stirring up rebellious sentiments among the slave, free black and prison populations. During his early years in Jamaica, there were recurring instances when George Liele demonstrated exceptional courage when faced with persecution and physical abuse by colonial authorities.

Finally Liele petitioned the colonial legislative body, which included representatives of the religious establishment, for the freedom to promote Christianity and to worship God according to his interpretation and understanding of the Bible. That audacious maneuver, indicative of his courage, was a quality that whites never expected a black man to possess. Liele's courage obviously generated a measure of respect in high places. Also, another factor must be introduced: notably that many in England and its colonies had also been exposed to the liberal Evangelical religious and political winds that had been spread by John Wesley and George Whitfield. The writings of Thomas Hobbes, an English social philosopher and author, also convincingly set forth that all men are divinely created in liberty and freedom. These gradually prevailing liberal ideas may have, over a period of years, been the reason severe persecution against Liele diminished.[44]

Three acres of land, at the corner of Victoria Avenue and Elletson Road at the east end of Kingston, was purchased for 770 dollars by Liele and his followers, in 1789. Construction of a brick meeting house to be known as the Windward Road Chapel was begun. The land adjacent to and around the building was used as a burial ground for the membership. To obtain money to complete the construction, George Liele, again using his skills and knowledge of dealing with whites, succeeded in obtaining the good will of several gentlemen of influence. One of them, a member of the colonial Jamaican Assembly named Stephen Cooke, was so impressed with Liele and the clarity of his vision, that he was moved to contact several friends in England to contribute money to help with the building effort.[45]

One of Cooke's friends was the Reverend John Rippon, pastor of the Carter Land Church in London and influential editor and publisher of the *Baptist Annual Register*. Rippon was also one of the founders of the Baptist Missionary Society. In a letter to Rippon, Liele reported that he had gathered a membership in Kingston, including a few whites, of nearly 350. Most were slaves whom he called "the poor Ethiopian Baptists of Jamaica." He urged Rippon to appeal to English Baptists to send the money needed to complete the church building. In that letter, Liele also claimed that there were about 1,500 people, including a few whites, free blacks and Creoles (racially mixed) living elsewhere in Kingston, Spanish Town and the country area near St. Andrews (the rural area and hill country north of Kingston) who had a relationship with a Baptist church. That may well have been the people about whom Mervyn C. Alleyne speculated when he wrote that in 1783 a group of "about 400 whites (Loyalist) families and between 4,000 and 5,000 of their Negro slaves" had come to Jamaica fleeing the war in the English colonies (of North America) of those initiated by those who wanted to establish a new nation totally free of English authority. Some of those people may have been associated previously with Baptist churches.[46] In a letter to John Rippon, Liele reported that he "had an English soldier as well as American blacks in his Kingston congregation."[47]

Over a period of years, Liele received money from the English Baptist to complete the construction in 1793. It was the first Baptist church on the island and also the "first dissenting chapel" to be built in Jamaica.[48] However, initially, the amount of money from the English Baptists was not enough to pay off the indebtedness incurred just to lay the foundation and raise the walls of the small (fifty-seven feet in length by thirty-seven feet in width) church building. Gayle reasons that when Liele was unable to satisfy his creditors, he was arrested by the magistrates and kept in prison for three years until the debt was paid.[49] Certainly having to spend time in "debtors prison" was common in late eighteenth century England and her colonies. Nevertheless, there may have been another reason for his arrest which will be discussed later. While he was in prison, Liele appointed his son, Paul, to preach

East Queen Street Baptist Church, Kingston.

Hanover Street Baptist Church, Kingston.

and help hold the Windward Road membership together. Paul Liele was unable to carry out his father's request.

When Liele was released from prison on March 10, 1807, basically because of the influence and intervention of an Anglican Rector, Dr. Thomas Rees, he found that the Windward Road Chapel membership had scattered. It is believed that the four deacons Pastor Liele had placed in charge with his son while he was in prison were responsible for the dispersion of the members. The role of one of those four deacons, a Jamaican born Creole class leader named Thomas Nicholas Swigle, will be discussed later. Two historic churches today in Kingston, East Queen Street Baptist Church, first organized by Swigle as Gully Chapel, and the Hanover Street Baptist Church claim founding members who were originally baptized by the Reverend Liele and were members of the Windward Road Chapel.[50]

Within thirty years, Baptist churches influenced by the ubiquitous George Liele were to be found in five of the twelve parishes (or districts) of Jamaica. By 1814, the membership of Liele related churches was estimated to be about eight thousand. With additional money from English Baptist supporters, Liele was able to complete the Windward Road Church, as has been noted previously, but also purchased property in Spanish Town, at that time, the capital of Jamaica. The property at Spanish Town contained a house which served as a meeting chapel and also included land designated for a graveyard.[51]

Although documentation has not surfaced, it is not unreasonable to believe that because of the many years of friendship Liele maintained with the pastor-publisher John Rippon and other influential English Baptists, he was probably invited to visit England, sometime between 1822 and 1826, to minister to a group of blacks who worshiped separately within the Carter's Land Church in the Soho section of London and appear as a person of historical fame at Baptist churches throughout the country. His contribution to the worldwide fellowship of Baptists should not, indeed cannot be underestimated, unremembered or neglected. As will be documented, Liele not only initiated the first contacts between Jamaican and English Baptists but he was, in fact, the most notable Baptist personage of the late eighteenth and early nineteenth centuries. His letters and attestations published by Rippon circulated throughout the international Baptist community for many years. Some of them may be reviewed at the Trask Library of the Andover Newton Theological School, in the Newton Center section of Boston, Massachusetts.

A Free School at Every Chapel

George Liele was the first Baptist missionary to establish churches in Jamaica which combined education with the spread of the Gospel. In every gathering, meeting house, chapel or church, he encouraged combining worship with teaching. Although he was a man only a few years removed from slavery and the recipient of a limited rudimentary exposure to reading and writing by the man who legally owned him and his family, Liele was, if not the first, the first known black church leader in Jamaica to recognize the urgency of teaching slaves and free blacks to read and write, the basis of an educational experience. Under his guidance, meeting houses and church buildings became centers which Liele called Free Schools to teach children to read the Bible and other things. The most developed church school was in Spanish Town.[52] That Liele was not punished for organizing church schools and emphasizing reading and writing may be due to the fact that while the Anglican Church's Society for the Propagation of the Gospel in Foreign Parts held no scruples against the system of slavery, the bishop of London had announced in March 1743 that in English colonies, country-born young Negroes would be purchased and instructed to read and understand the rudiments of Christianity so that they might in turn instruct all Negro and Indian children born in the colonies. Even though the efforts in colonial Carolina (and probably elsewhere) were resisted by angry white people, in Jamaica that Anglican policy may have been the reason Liele's church schools were ignored.[53] The Jamaican Assembly did, in 1806, pass a law prohibiting Christian teaching of any kind on plantations.

Liele developed teachers by identifying men in his congregations who showed evidence of high moral character, unusual leadership skills and possessed the ability to read. He personally trained and then appointed them as deacons to serve as teachers. Deacons were also used to assist him and other preachers during baptism and communion services. The dual focus, salvation and education continues throughout Jamaica. The fact that George Liele initiated and vigorously promoted those skills in Afro-Jamaican Baptist church settings is indicative of his unusual vision, insight and leadership skills.

The Baptist Class System

Another unique development of Liele's Baptist church movement was his adoption and modified use of the Class Meeting System originally developed by the Reverend John Wesley for Wesleyan Methodism. Wesley, universally regarded as the father of the modern Methodist Church movement, was a gifted eighteenth century preacher and evangelist with pre-eminent organizational skills. At first, he established societies consisting of converted (or saved) persons. "Those societies were divided into "bands" or groups . . . for mutual cultivation of the Christian life . . . On February 15, 1742, the society members were divided into classes of about twelve persons, each under a "class leader" charged to collect a penny weekly from each member. . . . Its advantages for spiritual oversight and mutual watch were soon even more apparent than its financial merits. It (the class system) . . . became one of the characteristic features of Methodism. . . ."[54]

Neither George Liele's many letters to John Rippon or other sources used to research this book reveal how the former slave preacher from colonial Georgia, whose religious life was totally circumscribed by the Baptist ministers who nurtured and ordained him, became knowledgeable about the Methodist class system. He certainly had not encountered any such administrative arrangement in the white Baptist churches or associational circles in which he was permitted to preach, teach or organize extemporaneously. Therefore, it is with a degree of certainty to conclude that Liele had no precedent for using the class system as a useful mechanism to develop strong Baptist churches in Jamaica. However, there is historical documentation that proves that the Reverend Thomas Coke laid the groundwork for the Methodist Episcopal Church in what is now the United States and the West Indies. He arrived in Jamaica in 1789.

Coke's plan for the establishment of missions effectively utilized the "class-meeting" structure and encouraged leadership development and utilization of the abilities of blacks, whites, and people of color.[55] George Liele's successes probably so interested Coke that he may have met with him to learn about evangelism among the slave and free black populations. At the same time, by a process of ecclesiastical reciprocity, Liele learned about the advantages of utilizing the class meeting concept and adapted it for use in his Baptist churches.

Liele seems to have demonstrated administrative creativity by appropriating and modifying certain features of the Wesleyan system to fit the need of independent (autonomous) Baptist churches. That adaptation became a very crucial factor in the development and growth of the fledgling Afro-Jamaican Baptist churches in Jamaica.

Liele divided his congregations into classes and appointed deacons as class leaders. The deacon was not only responsible for the spiritual care of each member (in his class) but in some instances may have been responsible for teaching and catechizing (a question and answer requirement). When authorized by George Liele, class leaders also exerted disciplinary measures over classes which met once every Monday. Mason Crum, writing about the development of the class system among slave churches in colonial Carolina, said, "The class meeting . . . lent itself admirably to the problems of slave conversion. . . . Here each member could speak and, if he desired, give his religious experience . . . The result was that it quickened interest in what the ministers (or leaders) were trying to do, gave personal opportunities for personal service, and provided a kind of clearing house for details of church membership."[56] For the slaves in Jamaica, it provided opportunities to share such issues and concerns as their treatment on various plantations. Slave unrest and revolts were certainly discussed and perhaps planned in those weekly class settings. A similar class system at the Hampstead African Methodist Episcopal Church in Charleston, South Carolina was used to recruit members and indoctrinate and train them to participate in a massive slave revolt in 1822. The class leader and organizer of the slave revolt was a free black, Gabriel Vesey.[57]

Although Liele was solely responsible for baptizing converts, church discipline and presiding over the Lord's Supper, he used class leaders (deacons) to assist him during evangelist services and to prepare new converts for baptism. In essence, the class system and its leaders provided the essential organizational ingredient for consistent church growth and the development of what came to be known as "Native" Baptist leadership. In 1993, 175 years after the congregation was organized by George Liele, the historic Phillippo (First) Baptist Church of Spanish Town reported that every member had been assigned to one of twenty-nine classes. "Each leader is responsible for leadership in Bible Study . . . in the community two Wednesdays per month, keeping a register of members, and reporting to the church on the Class' behalf. . . . "Monitoring Deacons" . . . are responsible for overseeing the activities of two or more classes."[58] Although Baptist churches in the United States under Jamaican leadership may use the class system to some extent, it may have only been duplicated in the Bahama Islands.

Deacons as class leaders often became influential church leaders. Some promoted the kind of serious division that occurred while the Reverend Liele was in prison because of debts incurred while attempting to construct the Windward Road Chapel. As has been noted, one of the deacons and school helpers Liele appointed to oversee his initial Kingston congregation and Free School was Thomas Nicholas Swigle. He was one of the first Creoles (persons of European parentage) in Jamaica to be identified with the Afro-Jamaican Baptist church movement. He convinced a number of the members to withdraw from Windward Road to organize another church. He also persuaded an Anglican clergyman, Dr.

Thomas Rees, to sanction his "call" to ministry and grant him a license to preach. That "surreptitious" but legal procedure that satisfied the Anglican Church and Jamaican colonial authorities may have been granted as an effort to diminish Liele's influence and popularity among slaves and free blacks. Swigle, on the other hand, obviously was a persuasive preacher with unusual leadership skills because he soon had a following of more than six hundred men and women. He called his meeting house St. John's Chapel and, like Liele, referred to his members as "the poor Ethiopian Baptists."[59]

NOTES

[39]Gayle, p. 11.
[40]"Letters Showing the Rise and Progress of Early Negro Churches in Georgia and West Indies," *Journal of Negro History I*, January 1916), pp. 70, 75.
[41]Curtin, p. 32.
[42]Gayle, p. 14.
[43]Mervyn C. Alleyne, *Roots of Jamaican Culture* (Kingston: University of West Indies Press, 1988), p. 89.
[44]Alleyne, p. 89.
[45]Gayle, pp. 17, 14.
[46]Alleyne, p. 89.
[47]Arthur Charles Dayfoot, *The Shaping Of The West Indian Church, 1492-1962* (Kingston: University of West Indies Press, 1999), p. 278.
[48]Holmes, p. 338.
[49]Gayle, p. 14.
[50]Ibid., p. 18-20.
[51]Ibid., p. 21.
[52]Ibid., p. 22.
[53]Crum, pp. 179, 180.
[54]Williston Walker, *A History of the Christian Church* (New York: Charles Scribner's Sons, 1970), pp. 460.
[55]Dayfoot, pp. 131-133.
[56]Crum, p. 218.
[57]Gayraud S. Wilmore, *Black Religion and Black Radicalism* (Garden City, New York: Doubleday & Company, 1972), p. 83.
[58]Phillippo Baptist Church Anniversary Booklet, p. 20.
[59]Turner, p. 10; Gayle, p. 22-24.

Chapter Four

MOSES BAKER: LIELE'S COLLEAGUE IN EVANGELISM

Extending Baptist Churches to Western Jamaica

Moses Baker was the man most often associated with George Liele. He was influenced, baptized and ordained as a Baptist preacher by Liele. Baker is honored as a pioneer Baptist preacher and as a founder of Native Baptist churches in Jamaica. (The Native Baptist movement will be discussed in the following chapter)

Baker and his family were among Loyalist refugees who left New York with other supporters of the King of England in 1783 and arrived in Kingston about the same time as Liele.[60] Baker had several advantages over many of the refugee blacks who sought to establish themselves as freemen in colonial Jamaica. Like George Liele, he could read and write and he was a barber by profession. He had also been a member of an Anglican Church in New York City and had been formally joined in marriage to Susannah Ashton by the rector, the Reverend W. Walters. Baker always confessed to friends, that although a church member, he was in reality, an unconverted churchman. Three years after arriving in Jamaica, his sight began to fail. Fortunately he found employment on a farm in Cambe County owned by a Quaker named Isaac Lascelles Winn.[61] During that period he became friends with an old black man, Cupid Welkin, who encouraged him to attend prayer meetings on the Winn estate led by a group of slaves who were followers of George Liele. In time, after he became completely blind, Baker was converted and baptized. Between the two men, a mutual friendship began that developed into an abiding respect for each other.[62] Baker and his family arrived in Delphi (about eleven miles southeast of Montero Bay in St. James Parish) in February 1788.

Obeah and Myalism were deeply rooted and pervasive among the slaves of the western areas of Jamaica. Christianity was almost nonexistent. Moravian missionaries had set up a Christian center at Bogue in St. Elizabeth Parish thirty-four years earlier but most of them died because of malaria, yellow fever or dysentery. Slaves had not been exposed to Christianity since.[63] Moses Baker was the first black man to promote Christianity in western Jamaica, and of course, the first black Baptist. But he was not welcomed by everyone. Two weeks after he arrived, one of the leading men who had listened to him teach and witness, "agreed that what he was saying was good, but he and . . . negroes . . . could not follow it . . . To make his point, he took Baker first to his own house and showed him bottles, horns, and other things employed in the working of witchcraft. He informed Baker that similar things could be found in homes of other Negroes . . . (Baker) . . . discovered that Negroes had up to five wives and . . . it was very difficult to enforce monogamy."[64]

Notwithstanding the difficulties, Baker was able to fall back on the preparation given him by George Liele. He demonstrated knowledge about the bible, church doctrine, the administration of the ordinances of baptism (held at nearby rivers) and communion, church organization and management. Combined with effective preaching, Baker soon organized churches on the Winn and other nearby estates. A British planter, Samuel Vaughn, who owned a plantation on the Jamaican North Coast, became his protector. Vaughn invited Baker to visit his estate and arranged for visits to the estates of other planters. He also donated land and timber for meeting houses.[65] Baker was effective in his missionary efforts because he was able to identify with the needs and aspirations of the rural slave population.

By 1814, in spite of being punished and imprisoned for not being duly qualified and authorized to preach to the slave population, Baker reported a membership of approximately five hundred people and several churches in an area where there had been none. Gayle believes that Baker not only laid a solid foundation for Baptist work in St. James, Westmoreland, Trelawny and Hanover Parishes, but the seed of the Gospel he planted is the reason western Jamaica still has some of the strongest Baptist churches in the island nation.[66]

Baker's pastoral and evangelistic efforts began to diminish as his age and failing health combined to rob him of physical stamina. He realized that if his work was to be sustained and developed, he had to have assistance. He shared his concern with his longtime friend, counselor and colleague, George Liele. Liele suggested that they write letters to be forwarded to the Baptist clergy in England. In previous correspondence, he had already informed them about evangelistic and church-planting efforts in western Jamaica and elsewhere. The British group, founders of the British Missionary Society (sometimes called London Missionary Society), included the Reverend John Ryland, President of Bristol College in Bristol, England and the Reverend John Rippon, Editor-Owner of the influential *Baptist Herald* which published religious news events in England and the English colonies.[67]

The letter from Liele and Baker reached the English Baptists sometime in 1813. In particular, it summarized Baker's struggle to plant (organize) and develop a significant Baptist witness in Western and Northwestern Jamaica in spite of his physical disabilities. Baker pleaded for both financial assistance and, most significantly, English missionaries to carry on and extend the work he had initiated twenty-six years previously. He emphasized the danger that the newly developed Christian faith of new slave converts might weaken under tremendous pressure and intimidation from the practitioners of Obeah and Myalism. Baker and Liele also wrote of the opportunities for Christian growth and Baptist witness.[68]

The letter to the British Baptists was timely for several reasons. Firstly, the leadership of the Baptist churches in England had already recognized that throughout the British colonies, especially West Africa, the African populations were not Christian. To focus their concern, they had only recently formed the British Missionary Society. Many were already engaged in the

British Anti-Slavery Society, crusading for the abolition of the slave trade and slavery itself. Secondly, although from its inception, the evangelistic efforts of the fledgling mission organization was West Africa, India and Burma, the members of the Society were aware (because of Liele's correspondence) that groups of Afro-Jamaican Baptists were being gathered from among the slaves as the result of black preachers from North America, particularly a free black named George Liele. They also knew that one of Liele's associates, a mulatto barber, Moses Baker, was laboring, with surprising results, in Western Jamaica.[69] Thirdly, the British Missionary Society was aware that laws passed by the colonial Assembly had closed all churches for slaves and free blacks in Kingston. Magistrates were refusing to license any missionary or preacher, white or black, involved with the slave community. In addition, the magistrates had "established the right to insist on due qualifications" before granting any preacher a license. In effect, there was no place in the system for Baptist preachers, especially if they were black. A part of the credential process was that preachers had to be accredited by ministers of a recognized (white, non-Baptist) church denomination. The chapel constructed by George Baker was being used as a hospital. Even though some blacks like Liele and Baker were being permitted to resume religious work on the estates of a few planters, for the most part, the Afro-Jamaican Baptist Church movement had ceased to develop.[70]

The initial response of the British Missionary Society (BMS) was to send missionaries to assist Liele, Baker and Thomas Swigle. However, aware that all preaching to slaves by whites and blacks had been terminated, the BMS tabled Baker's request. But later that same year, a missionary was commissioned to assist Baker in Western Jamaica and eventually assume most of his responsibilities. A pattern of 'assistance' was established that was followed by other Afro-Jamaican Baptist congregations throughout Jamaica. However, as more and more English missionaries arrived and assumed leadership roles, some congregations disintegrated. The members of those churches were unable or unwilling to respond to the more formal English worship style. Other congregations became independent Baptist-type sects under their own "home grown" pastoral leadership like Thomas Swigle, which had more traditional and familiar "free" worship patterns. Those Baptist-type groups became known as Native Baptists.[71]

Notes

[60] Sherlock and Bennett, p. 203.
[61] Gayle, p. 25.
[62] Ibid., p. 27.
[63] Sherlock and Bennett, p. 179.
[64] Gayle, p. 29.
[65] Turner, p. 22
[66] Gayle, p. 30
[67] Earnest A. Payne, *Freedom In Jamaica* (London: The Carey Press, 1833), pp. 11, 19.
[68] Ibid., p 19.
[69] Ibid., pp. 17, 18.
[70] Turner, p. 17.
[71] Ibid., p. 17.

Chapter Five

NATIVE BAPTISTS: SPIRIT CHRISTIANS

The Africanization of Baptist Christianity

Ideas and beliefs about the spirit world, the inherent quality or basic constitution of God, the ultimate destiny of man and the question of what constitutes a family, were questions the slaves and free blacks had to reconsider as the teaching of English missionaries began to challenge their belief systems. Their response was reflected paradoxically by the growth of Baptist mission churches with their church-related schools as well as the development and proliferation of splinter "church" groups or sects. The new sect-type churches reflected various coalitions and combinations of Christian, Baptist and Neo-African religious beliefs that slave preachers, and sometimes themselves, developed. George Simpson, a perceptive religious sociologist, introduces the argument that "the shift to religious cults of one kind or another as coming in the first instance from the nature of the slavery system and the system that followed it, and the social, economic, and political treatment which those at the bottom of these systems receive. Over time, these conditions modified character in a stressful direction, and those who were most sensitive to the stress advanced new religious and secular systems to deal with their anxiety. . . . Successful religions spread and persist after the conditions which gave birth to them have changed, or changes to some extent. . . ."[72] In the same way, slave religion modified African religions and Christianity to create Neo-African religious systems such as Myalism or Vodun.

The modified cult groups in Jamaica during the early nineteenth century were generally known as Native Baptists or Spirit Christians. The term, 'Native Baptists' was clearly generic, a descriptive term for religious forms of worship that sometimes could hardly be designated as Baptist or Christian. However, those forms of worship clearly reflected the needs of the enslaved people of Jamaica much more closely than the religion of the orthodox English Baptist missionaries or even George Liele whose more non-agitative "pacifist" style of playing it safe in a hostile and alien environment, in colonial Georgia and Jamaica, won the approval and admiration of white Baptists.[73] (Liele's legacy as a so-called pacifist will be examined in more detail in subsequent discussions.)

From the beginning, especially in the rural areas of western Jamaica, the membership of Baptist churches and missions reflected a blending (syncretism) of Christian and Neo-African religious beliefs. The Christianity and worship of slaves and free blacks of Baptist churches in cities such as Kingston, Spanish Town and Montego Bay was more orthodox and European theologically, reflecting the influence of George Liele and his North American religious roots, and later, the English missionaries. Turner points out that the splintering, division and merging among the Baptists into unorthodox church groups accelerated during the period when black and white 'licensed' preachers were forbidden to preach to slaves. Variations of Baptist religious groups occurred everywhere.[74]

George Liele attempted to keep his congregations as "orthodox" as possible, organized along lines similar to those of colonial Baptist churches. But even he was not excluded from having to confront the development of unorthodoxy among groups of members whose illiteracy and misunderstanding was more profound. Even some of the preachers he had personally ordained were either forced or encouraged to mix elements of Christianity and Baptist doctrine with Neo-African practices. One of those was Thomas Nicholas Swigle, Baptist deacon and class leader in the Windward Road Chapel. Swigle was a very intelligent man whom Liele had made church overseer when he was jailed. Even Moses

Baker modified his Baptist orthodoxy. It may have been that his physical condition seriously reduced his ability to remain a strong, orthodox, commanding Baptist church leader. He had to confront and even accept internal dissension within his congregations in Western Jamaica where members had always included those who believed in armed slave uprisings and were adherents of witchcraft.

Others, teachers, class leaders and "counselors" of new converts became spiritual guides, taking positions equivalent to leadership in Myal groups. In their mixed roles, part Christian and Baptist and part Myal, their power over church classes sometimes became authoritarian to the point of being tyrannical. Their power extended beyond simple religious matters. In those churches where the minister (or preacher) was not strong and charismatic, loosely federated classes tended to break off to follow other leaders who formed new Native Baptist church cults.[75]

Some church leaders, groups and classes began to emphasize "spirit" or "spirits" rather than the Holy Spirit. Members, or followers, had to be possessed (ridden) by one or more spirits before the leader or preacher would baptize them. Certain ceremonial services such as fasting and interpreting dreams were required to invoke spirit-possession. In some instances, as Curtin explains, even the position of Jesus Christ was subordinated to emphasize the role of the New Testament John the Baptist, giving the baptism service a new, completely different, spiritual doctrinal emphasis. Only the independent organizational structure (the autonomy of each church) and the exhortation or preaching, both features of the early independent Baptist Church movement, were retained and incorporated into Native Baptist policy and worship.[76]

A major modification of the original teaching of George Liele that became a dominant feature of the Native Baptists was their emphasis of social and political matters. One of the unfortunate criticisms of George Liele by those who claim to have evaluated his preaching and ministries in colonial Georgia and Jamaica has been that he never used his position and influence to attack the system of slavery, the conditions of poverty and political powerlessness, nor did he join with others who fought for physical emancipation and freedom with justice for the under classes. This kind of criticism of Liele will be examined and discredited in succeeding chapters. Meanwhile, as has been noted, while the slaves from West Africa retained strong religious traditions, their social and political organizations had been destroyed as they were forcefully and systematically separated by tribe, clan and family prior to, during and following the terror and suffering filled Middle Passage. This vacuum had been filled to some degree by the stringent and sterile plantation system and Neo-African religions such as Obeah and Myalism. The ceremonies and administrations of the Obeah and Myal men provided slaves with a sense of belonging, security, even hope in their present world and in the next.

Suddenly, slaves were exposed to Native Baptist leaders who built their influence by combining the power of Christianity which seemed to protect white people (and their slave masters) so effectively with the influence and power of the traditional African gods and spirits with their mixture or combination of possession and intimidation. The power sources of the Native Baptist preachers tended to reinforce each other. Sherlock and Bennett note that "slave drivers, boilers, masons, and other plantation officials became leaders in the Afro-Christian cults under the title of assistant preacher or class leader. . . ."[77]

For approximately forty years, the religious movement that was orthodox Baptist Christianity begun by George Liele in 1783, and to some degree, Christianity itself, was reinterpreted and modified by Native Baptist preachers. New models of Baptist churches emerged. Church organizations were reorganized, modified and re-created in the loosely knit Native Baptist movement throughout Jamaica. By 1830, that evolution process, more or less Christian, depending on the leadership of a particular group, was a thoroughly integrated part of the culture of the overwhelming majority of Afro-Jamaicans. The movement became a religion, competing with the Christianity preached and taught by Anglican, Roman Catholic Europeans and the English and orthodox African Baptist preachers like George Liele. Even later, when Afro-Jamaicans joined British missionary led Baptist churches, men with Myal connections often held class leader-deacon positions, especially in the Western parishes such as Trelawny, Hanover and St. James.[78] By 1865, Native Baptists outnumbered regular (orthodox) Baptists in the capital city of Kingston but were never given special status in the official censuses published by the Jamaican governments.[79]

NOTES

[72]Simpson, p. 53.

[73]Winston Arthur Lawson, *Religion and Race: African and European Roots in Conflict—A Jamaican Testament*, (New York: Peter Lang Publishing, Inc., 1996), p 29.

[74]Turner, p. 58

[75]Curtin, p. 33

[76]Ibid., p. 34.

[77]Sherlock and Bennett, p. 181.

[78]Curtin, p. 34.

[79]*Freedom To Be: The Abolition of Slavery in Jamaica and its Aftermath*, second ed. (Kingston: National Library of Jamaica, p. 56.

Chapter Six

THE BRITISH MISSIONARY SOCIETY

Early English Missionary Leadership

The British Missionary Society (a.k.a. the B.M.S. and the London Missionary Society) was founded by preachers, educators and religious writers. All had been influenced by the religious revival in England known as the Evangelical Movement that was strongly affected by the preaching of the Wesley brothers, John and Charles, and George Whitfield. As Sherlock and Bennett point out, "So widespread and so fervent was the religious revival that by the 1790s the old dissenting churches, such as the Baptists, were having their own religious revival."[80]

Juxtaposed and woven into the proclamations of the Wesley brothers, Whitfield and others were some of the radical ideas emanating from the European period known as the Enlightenment. Precipitated by the writings of two Frenchmen, Francois-Marie Voltaire and Jean-Jacques Rousseau, the Enlightenment was an intellectual awakening during the 1760's. Ideas such as (national) governments being bound to guarantee the rights and liberties of all subjects, freedom of speech and religion, equality of all people regardless of status or condition, began to influence rulers of governments and religious bodies. "Freedom, the rights of man, equality and brotherhood became realities."[81]

The group of Baptists at the B.M.S. headquarters in Northamptonshire, England decided to send missionaries to Jamaica in response to a letter from George Liele and Moses

Baker urgently requesting help. The missionaries who were selected to go were commissioned by the Society and instructed to recognize, support and augment the successful Baptist mission and church planting development initiative already established and nurtured by the two black pioneer evangelists. The missionaries were also informed that both Liele and George were men of outstanding character and conduct who had been tested by the trials of racial and religious persecution and the fire of imprisonment and multiple forms of physical duress. Against great adversity, the pioneer preachers had succeeded in planting seeds of the Baptist denomination, organizing and constructing church houses (worship centers) and schools in many parts of Jamaica while being faithful to the teachings of the Bible and Baptist principles.

Each missionary was also warned that the colonial land owners and planters and the local governing authorities in Jamaica had already labeled the Baptist leaders as radical, and that, along with legal problems, they would have difficulty getting permission to preach or minister to the slave population. One of the missionaries commissioned was the twenty-five-year-old John Rowe. After being advised to give Moses Baker the precedence befitting an elder, Rowe and his wife sailed from Bristol, England on December 31, 1813. The first English missionary arrived at Montego Bay, St. James Parish in western Jamaica on February 23, 1814, thirty years after George Liele reached Kingston and organized the first Baptist chapel in 1784. Rowe's arrival was described in the local newspaper called the *St. James Parish Register* as an "Anabaptist missionary," identifying one who believed in only baptizing adults.[82] Of course, in 1782, no newspaper had reported the arrival of an indentured black man from the British colony of Georgia named George Liele.

Eventually, Rowe took over George Baker's church groups and mission development responsibilities. Stanley notes that Rowe "found Baker's slave congregation in serious disarray. The law against Christian preaching to slaves had prevented Baker from teaching his flock for eight years; there had been no baptisms for over three years, and no celebration of the Lord's Supper for more than ten. Nevertheless, it is estimated that total Baptist membership on the island was about 8,000. A Moravian missionary praised Baker in 1818 as a 'blessed and active servant of God.'"[83]

George E. Simpson acknowledges the arrival of the Reverend Rowe and other British missionaries who followed him with the following tribute. "Thirty years after Liele's arrival in Jamaica, the British Missionary Society began to send out missionaries. . . ." Many "were stricken with malaria and other diseases, and served an average of three years. . . ." By 1831, the influx of talented British Baptist preachers had taken over the leadership of most Baptist congregations throughout Jamaica. Mission church leadership passed from black to white, a phenomena that endured in mission-related churches for more than one hundred forty years.[84]

In less than fifteen years after the first British missionary arrived in Jamaica, both George Liele and Moses Baker were dead. The year of Liele's death is questionable, either 1825 or 1828. William Knob, a British missionary who arrived in Jamaica in 1825, was present at his funeral.[85] The location of Liele's grave is also unknown, but Moses Baker was buried in the old Salters Hill Baptist Church in Kingston.

In addition to the ministries of Moses Baker, Missionary John Rowe also organized a Baptist mission in Falmouth about eighteen miles from Montego Bay in Trelawny Parish. In less than two years and six months, he was replaced by the Reverend William Knibb who is recognized as the founder of the Falmouth Baptist Church. Knibb only lived in Jamaica two months but even then expressed his interest in seeing the British Missionary Society extend its evangelistic efforts to the island of Haiti. The flow of young British missionaries continued after Knibb, and worship services and schools for slaves and free blacks continued in Falmouth and reopened in Kingston and Spanish Town even as the opposition of the planters and colonial officials toward them intensified. Eugene D. Genovese notes, that "The living history of the . . . (established) . . . church has been primarily a history of submission to class stratification and the powers that be." But Genovese concluded, "there has remained . . . a legacy of resistance . . . The gods must surely enjoy their joke. Christianity's greatest bequest to western civilization lies in its doctrines of spiritual freedom and equality before God . . . . Christianity offered to the oppressed and the despised the image of God crucified by power, greed, and malice and yet, in the end resurrected, triumphant, and redeeming the faithful."[86] Genovese' conclusion is justified when one examines the fruits of the preaching, militant actions and life commitments of Baptist preachers such as the anti-Puritan, Roger Williams (founder of the first Baptist Church in America) and the civil rights and peace activist, Dr. Martin Luther King, Jr.

Mary Turney was historically perceptive when she observed that for those Afro-Jamaicans who were exposed to the preaching, Bible study and doctrine presented by the Baptists, the concept of the autonomy of each Baptist church provoked great interest. "Mission activities and organization provided, within the confines of church membership, small concrete examples of the equality of the slave and free in Christian fellowship. . . ." It ". . . developed new leadership elements among the slaves, and stimulated the network of religious meetings that proved capable of providing the organizational groundwork for the 1831 rebellion . . . .The missionaries themselves provided the slaves with a new model of authority . . . based . . . on example and persuasion . . . and prepared (the slaves) to challenge their masters, even (though) they never lifted their eyes from the hoe as the missionaries went by."[87]

When British Missionary, Thomas Burchell, arrived in Jamaica in 1823, he was initially denied a licensed to peach. Nevertheless, he worked with a church group of slaves in Northwestern Jamaica that had been organized by Moses Baker. Burchell led them in building the Montego Bay Baptist Mission.[88] (The words "mission church" was a euphemism for "church for slaves.") Within a few years, it became one of the most famous (or infamous) churches in Jamaica. In January 1832, Burchell was accused of encouraging slaves of his church and the surrounding Trelawny Parish area to rebel against the land owners and slave holders and their infamous system of involuntary servitude. Although he was eventually declared to be innocent of the charges that he had incited the rebellion, one spiritual descendent of George Liele and George Baker, a deacon and class leader of the Montego Bay Baptist Church, was not. His name was Samuel (Sam) Sharpe. Sharpe was also a Native Baptist church leader and leader of one of the major slave uprisings and revolts in Jamaica.

Samuel (Sam) Sharpe: Baptist Deacon, Class-Leader and National Hero

The slave, Sam Sharpe, possessed a keen intellect and an ambitious nature. He taught himself to read and write. His owners recognized and appreciated his leadership qualities on the plantation and rewarded him with special privileges. After he was influenced and converted by the preaching of Moses Baker, Sharpe was given a practical licensed to travel and preach at will with limited work responsibilities. Baker made him a class leader. When Thomas Burchell took over the group, Sharpe became a follower. He seems to have quickly recognized the political dynamic of Christian teaching. It is said that he quoted the words of Matthew 6:24, "No man can serve two masters" so frequently that they became a slogan among the slaves. Burchell did not know that Sharpe was dually aligned, actively involved in the Native Baptist movement in Montego Bay and surrounding Trelawny Parish and a member of an orthodox Christian church. Already a class leader, Missionary Burchell made him his chief deacon.[89] The members of both the Christian Baptist and Native Baptist groups affectionately called him "Daddy" or "Ruler" Sharpe "not only because of his charismatic and saintly character but because of his almost unique mobility."[90]

For several months prior to December 1831, conflicting rumors swept through western Jamaica, suggesting that "brown already free, black soon." Emancipation would come if it was fought for, because "Freedom was coming in a paper from the king by the hand of the Baptist Missionary Burchell."[91] Daddy Sharpe convinced other class leaders and plantation slave drivers that a protest or strike was necessary. Following his instructions, preparations for the protest were combined with religious meetings. Large numbers of slaves met at twenty-two various orthodox Christian churches (eleven Baptist, three Presbyterian, three Wesleyan Methodist, and five Moravian) and an unknown number of Myal chapels. His stature as a leader was supported by the fact that Baptist influence in the area was very strong. Also, he was the head deacon and class leader in the church led by the influential Reverend Thomas Burchell and most knew that he was a leader in Native Baptist circles also. Knowing that the white planters and their families would be away, in Kingston or elsewhere, celebrating the Christmas holidays, the slaves bound themselves (by placing their hands on a Bible and uttering an oath that combined Christian and African religious traditions) not to work after Christmas as slaves but to assert their claim to freedom and to be faithful to each other. They also vowed that if any attempt was made to force them to work as slaves, they would fight for their freedom.

On December 28, 1831, the day after the Christmas holidays ended and harvesting the sugar cane was scheduled to begin, tens of thousands of slaves refused to go to the fields. When the English missionary pastors were informed of the revolt by frightened members, they called church meetings and preached and spoke against the revolt. Their warnings were largely ignored. Passive slave resistance quickly became a full insurrection. Slaves burned barns, houses and the fields of sugar cane. At least fifteen whites and more than four hundred and eighty slaves, including Sam (Daddy) Sharpe, were captured, flogged and executed.[92] It is reported that "every rebel, leaders and led, walked to the scaffold 'calm and undismayed' . . . with dignified bearing of men untroubled as to the justice of their cause . . . They rebelled to change the society they know and claim . . . the right to wages for work on the plantations . . . ."[93]

The Reverend Moses Baker was the first person Sharpe heard preach and was doubtlessly greatly influenced by him. From Baker, Sharpe received the impetus for political awareness that led him to become the first Afro-Jamaican "Christian" revolutionary and freedom fighter. Baker was admired and respected by his mentor, George Liele as well as the leaders of the British Missionary Society who praised him for his commitment to orthodox Christian doctrine. What is not certain, is whether he was also an advocate for slave rebellion in its extreme form. The answer to that question may be discerned in an amalgam of the following foci.

First, even though Moses Baker was preached to and taught fundamental Christian orthodox interpretations of the Bible and Baptist doctrine by his mentor and friend, the black church pioneer, George Liele, their early formative years were different. Liele's religious beginnings were associated with a restrictive slave plantation church religion while he was encouraged by a paternal slave owner who approved of his and other slave's spirituality and intellect. Having proven himself to the man who owned him, Liele was then affirmed by a white evangelical missionary preacher who verified his "call to ministry" and then promoted his ordination by other Caucasian Baptist preachers, some of whom probably owned slaves.

George Baker's formative years were different. He grew up in a more contemporary environment of a northern metropolitan community where he earned his living as a barber, catering to Caucasian clientele. He attended but was not, by his own admission, a conscientious member of an Anglican Church in the New York City area. He had not been exposed to the preaching of "fire and brimstone" Baptists. In fact, Baker joked about his 'un-Christian' life and confessed that his church connection had not affected his life style at all. In short, Baker's approach to Christian ministry was probably more practical and therefore more easily receptive of a social gospel than the orthodox Biblical evangelical approach of his mentor, George Liele.

Second, Baker may have heard Liele read and discuss passages from the New Testament which contained liberation and justice themes such as Galatians 3:28 that reads, in the King James translation, "There is neither Jew nor Greek, there is neither bond nor free, there is neither male nor female for ye are one in Christ Jesus."

Or perhaps it was a combination of stimuli that came to bear on Sam Sharpe: the less orthodox preaching and teaching of his first pastor, Moses Baker, the dubious encouragement from British missionaries, and the strong appeal of the Afro-centered social dogma that he encountered in Myal meetings. All of those concepts merging in Sharpe's mind created thoughts and ideas that drove him to inspire passionately fellow slaves into confrontation even against those who had been kind to him personally. Under his leadership, the slaves in north- western Jamaica revolted against the status quo to gain economic equity and freedom. The revolt is known as the Christmas Day Revolt or Baptist War.

One result of the revolt was that Missionary Thomas Burchell, pastor of the Montego Bay Baptist Mission Church was falsely accused by the white slave owning planters of encouraging the slaves. Arrested, he narrowly escaped being lynched by the incensed authorities, Burchell was forced to return to England. He and another missionary sent back to England by other British missionaries in Jamaica, joined together to help the British Missionary Society and the British Abolitionist movement promote public sentiment against slavery in the colonies and overcome the opposition of colonial sugar planters.

Sam Sharpe was executed for his leadership role in the Baptist War. But ten months later, in August 1832, the English Parliament passed a resolution that was signed into law by the King of England abolishing slavery in Jamaica and all other British colonies. One hundred and forty-two years later, October 1974, an independent Jamaica declared Samuel "Daddy" Sharpe a national hero for his decisive contribution to Jamaican freedom and independence.[94] The Baptist Deacon is remembered by a grateful Jamaican people but the name of the man whose preaching and vision planted the seeds of the Baptist church movement that ultimately produced, not one, but three national heroes, is mentioned only in a few Baptist churches. On the other hand, the man who brought church to Jamaica, the pioneer and founder, George Liele, is forgotten and unknown.

NOTES

[80]Sherlock and Bennett, pp. 177, 178.
[81]Ibid., p. 183.
[82]Payne, pp. 18, 19.
[83]Brian Stanley, *The History of the Baptist Missionary Society (1792-1992)* (Edinburgh: T & T Clark, 1992), p. 70.
[84]Simpson, p. 42.
[85]Gayle, p. 32.
[86]Genovese, pp. 163, 165.
[87]Turner, pp. 94, 95.
[88]Ibid., p. 108.
[89]Ibid., pp. 152, 153.
[90]Michael Craton, *Testing The Chains* (Ithaca: Cornell University Press, 1982), p. 299.
[91]Ibid., p. 295.
[92]Payne, pp. 27, 28; Sherlock and Bennett, p. 227.
[93]Turner, pp. 162, 163.
[94]Payne, pp. 42, 43; *The Gleaner*, p. 117.

Chapter Seven

THE LEGACY OF GEORGE LIELE: NON-VIOLENT ACTIVISM

Liele: Pacifier or Passive Resister

The legacy of George Liele, at this point in history, seems to be a "mixed bag" by those historians, religious writers, and church persons who know anything about him mainly because his life and achievements have not been fully reported or accurately and fairly evaluated. One African-American historian, Charles Hamilton, concluded that George Liele was an obsequious type of slave preachers he called pacifiers because he was one of those who "admonished their fellow slaves to be obedient, loyal to their masters and to endure the pains and problems of this life and to look forward to better things in the life hereafter." The Jamaican slave masters and planters, Hamilton argued, "did not need to employ an assistant nor to make use of the whip . . . (because their) . . . slaves were industrious and obedient . . ." because of Liele's preaching and teaching.[95]

Of course, if Hamilton and other critics had written about Liele in light of the information that has been uncovered within the last thirty years, they would have discovered that there are historical facts which significantly discredit Liele's "pacifier" label. In the first place, they would have learned that Jamaican slave owners, planters, Anglican church leaders, and the colonial assembly had Liele arrested and physically abused on many occasions because they were certain he was a trouble maker preaching sedition and rebellion. He was frequently sentenced to long periods in prison by "unsympathetic" magistrates.

Pioneer Preachers in Paradise

Dr. Gayraud Wilmore, a noted historian and religious educator, contends that even the pacifist preacher "was most relevant to this world when he was telling his congregation what to expect in the next one precisely because he whetted appetites for what everyone knew whites were undeservedly enjoying in the here and now . . . .To have suffered the indignities in the name of Jesus Christ, as was the case of Andrew Bryan and George Liele, could have increased the preachers' conviction that if whites so desperately tried to curb its proclamation, the gospel must have something very important to do with the freedom and well-being of blacks."[96]

A second insight about slave preachers was made by the reputable historian, Eugene D. Genovese. In eloquent and unforgettable words, he wrote "The religious tradition to which the Afro-American slaves fell heir and to which they contributed more than has yet been generally recognized (was) . . . by no means unambiguously inspired docility and blind submission . . . .In their own way the slaves demonstrated that, whatever the full truth or falsity of Christianity, it spoke for all humanity when it proclaimed the freedom and inviolability of the human soul . . . Even . . . diluted and perverted Protestantism lent itself, in various subtle but discernible ways, to the creation of a proto-national black consciousness."[97]

Third, the rationale and conclusions of Sherlock and Bennett, two distinguished historians, should be seriously considered. "The Evangelical Movement exerted a powerful influence in Jamaica through two black preachers, George Liele and Moses Baker . . . .Liele's preaching attracted large numbers of people, and the government prosecuted him for uttering seditious words. . . . They did two things that neither Moravians nor the English Baptists and Methodist missionaries who came after them, could have done. . . .Through their preaching, George Liele and Moses Baker defined the mission of the Christian Church in Jamaica and gave it a system of organization based on small chapels and deacons. . . . Further . . . because they had experienced slavery, (they) passed on a tradition of a church where African-Jamaicans were at home and participated both in managing its religious affairs and also in maintaining the principles of freedom, equality, and brotherhood. In maintaining this tradition, William Knibb and his colleagues were indispensable, *but the first steps were taken by Liele and Baker . . . and carried on by . . . George William Gordon . . . and Paul Bogle."* (Italics author's)[98]

Fourth, the cogent arguments of the Jamaican-American theologian and educator, Winston A. Lawson, provides what may be the most conclusive resolution to the discussion about whether the pioneer Baptist preacher, George Liele, was a pacifier or passive resister type of slave preacher or preacher to slaves. Lawson discovered that "the first time this black preacher (Liele) addressed his fellow people of African descent in Jamaica, he took for his text Paul's poignant words, written from a jail where he was in chains for preaching the gospel of love and justice. "Brethren, my heart's desire and prayer for Israel is that they might be saved." (Romans 10:1). Unlike the missionaries whom he would later invite to help him and his colleague, Moses Baker . . . . Liele did not employ a literalist and pie in the sky by and by interpretation of the Bible." Using the opinion of Noel Leo Erskine as a reference source, Lawson concludes that "From this very first recorded exposition by him, he immediately contextualized his interpretation and made the provocative connection between the predicament of Black people in Jamaica and that of Israel in Egypt. . . ."[99] Lawson continues about Liele, ". . . His radical plea was that they find liberation for their entire beings, (souls and bodies) in that historical context of oppression and uprootedness. It is not surprising that he was imprisoned for having preached such an "insurrectionary" sermon for which . . . the prosecution's charge was "sedition.""[100]

When one combines the arguments of these highly regarded church historians and religious scholars, there is but one conclusion, namely that George Liele may have been guilty only of maximizing his political skills to placate the colonial authorities while dedicating his life to lifting a down trodden people to a higher level, spiritually and educationally. One has to conclude, "playing with the hand he had been dealt" he played the game with great skill and finesse. The Afro-Jamaicans needed the special creative organizing gifts of a George Liele as well as the unconditional confrontation to the unjust system of slavery and post-emancipation that was provided by Samuel (Deacon) Sharpe, George William Gordon and Paul Bogle. All Jamaicans are indebted to him, including Sharpe, Gordon and Bogle, for the Afro-Jamaican Baptist church system which he organized because it provided the vehicle by which they were able to develop and maximize their leadership careers as Native Baptist preachers.

The Gordon-Bogle Morant Bay Revolt

As was true of the emancipated thousands of black slaves in the United States, once the euphoria of freedom passed, the new freedmen in Jamaica were confronted with the disparity between emancipation and concrete meaningful freedom. The Reverend Edward Undershill, secretary of the British Missionary Society aptly described the conditions of the newly freed Jamaican, when he wrote, "the extreme poverty of the people . . . left them no alternative but to steal or starve." He predicted the "entire failure of the island" unless something was done to create employment and in general, to alleviate the "ragged and even naked condition" of vast numbers of the formerly enslaved population."[101] In 1865, two Baptist preachers, George William Gordon and Paul Bogle, encouraged the newly freed people "towards political liberty by championing resistance to white minority oppression that divorced morality from the exercise of power."[102]

George Gordon was born a slave, the son of a quadroon slave woman and a white estate manager. His father gave his light-skinned son his freedom at an early age. When he was twenty-nine, and already a successful business man, Gordon succeeded in being elected to the Jamaican Assembly. Although raised in the Anglican Church, he was influenced by the preaching, teaching and life example of the British missionary pastor, James Phillippo of Spanish Town. Under Phillippo's guidance, Gordon was immersed and began to travel to other Baptist mission churches to preach and offer counsel. He was soon organizing other church groups. At age forty-nine, in 1860, he became a Native Baptist minister, establishing three independent Native Baptist chapels at Barth, Spring Gardens and Kingston. He did not, however, discontinue his association with the British missionary-led Baptists or other traditional Christian denominations. As a veteran member of the Jamaican Assembly, he championed the cause of the black and brown (mulatto) poor of Jamaica.[103]

An Afro-Jamaican named Paul Bogle was influenced by Gordon. Bogle was an independent farmer who was converted under Gordon's peaching. He became a member of a Native Baptist church organized by the Reverend George Gordon in Kingston. Gordon recognized the charismatic leadership qualities of the younger Bogle and ordained him as a deacon and church leader. In a short time, Bogle organized his own church group and built a chapel on his land at Stoney Gut. He too, blended Christian and Myal (African-Christian) beliefs and values with the context of strong religious militancy. T. C. Holt wrote, "Central to its functioning was a remarkable relationship between Bogle and George William Gordon . . . part political and religious alliance, part friendship, their relationship was founded in resistance."[104] Together, they transformed a wide-ranging series of local protests into a campaign for civil liberty. Their preaching and teaching gave their campaign the moral force and ethical sanction that clarified a sense of purpose and continuity for the masses. They successfully identified the basic concepts of good government for the newly emancipated black peasant folk who chose to assert their right to political liberty and justice guided by religious principles.[105]

In October 1865, several hundred men and women, gathered under the guise of celebrating the traditional festival of Jonkonnu carnival, but carrying cutlasses and sharpened sticks and a red flag as their symbol of solidarity, danced to the sound of beating drums to the court house in the fishing village of Morant Bay. Volunteer white militia fired on them and the marchers responded violently, burning the jail, releasing the prisoners and setting fire to several buildings. After a week of bloody fighting and many deaths, Paul Bogel and George Gordon were court-martialed and hanged. The uprising highlights further evidence "of the symbiotic relationship between socio-political protest and Afro-Christianity," where Christianity, Myalism and Obeah segued. "At least one accredited Obeah man, Arthur Wellington, took part in the uprising and was shot and decapitated . . . the oath taken by the insurgents—kissing the Bible and drinking a mixture of rum and gunpowder—a characteristic mixture of Christianity and Myalism."[106]

One year later, the planter oligarchy surrendered the right of government when Jamaica became a Crown colony. For almost one hundred years, the unrepresented people could expect the direct protection of the Crown (King and Queen) of England. The change, more symbolic than meaningful, and the dynamics of social and political improvements, had been gained under the leadership of Afro-Jamaicans, not British missionary Baptist church leaders. "Full political representation through universal adult suffrage and the secret ballot" was not achieved until eighty years later, in 1945.[107]

Both Gordon and Bogle, along with Sam Sharpe, three courageous freedom loving Baptist deacon-preacher-pastors who were directly and indirectly influenced by the organizational skills and vision of the former slave and first black Baptist missionary from British colonial America named George Liele, have been acclaimed National Heroes of Jamaica.

Once again we are reminded that the Native Baptist leadership of Jamaica is just another example of the continuing ability of Africans living in the western hemisphere to adapt both Christianity and African religions to form practical theological forms that are the most helpful to them in light of their existential oppressive situations and circumstances. A rallying cry of grass-roots political leaders for many years was, "Remember the Morant War."

NOTES

[95] Charles V. Hamilton, *The Black Preacher in America* (New York City: William Morrow Company, 1972), pp. 45-47.

[96] Wilmore, pp. 67-68.

[97] Genovese, pp. 166-167.

[98] Sherlock and Bennett, pp. 180-182.

[99] Lawson, pp. 74-75; Noel Erskine, *The Black Reformed Church* (New York: Reformed Church Press, 1978), p. 41.

[100] Lawson, p. 75; Beverly Brown, "George Liele: Black Baptist and Pan-Africanist, 1750-1826," *Savacou Fol.* 11?12: September 1975, p. 60.

[101] Burton, p. 108.

[102] Ibid., p. 246.

[103] Sherlock and Bennett, pp. 246-249.

[104] Ibid., p. 247.

[105] Ibid., p. 246-247.

[106] Ibid., p. 250.

[107] Ibid., pp. 112-113.

Chapter Eight

THE LIELE LEGACY: FREE EDUCATION

Free Chapel Schools to Calabar College

The Baptists were the first to place the Bible in Afro-Jamaican hands. Whenever and wherever the Reverend George Liele organized a church or purchased land, his plan called for two things: (1) a meeting house or a church and always a Free School to teach all children to read and write; and (2) a grave yard to bury members who died. In his international paper, the editor of the *Baptist Annual Register* and one of the founders of the British Missionary Society writing about Liele said, "He can be said to be one of the early pioneers of education among slaves in Jamaica. Deacons served . . . as educators. . . . Under his leadership a school . . . was established for both free and slave children. Small groups under the tutelage of selected teachers were organized in various parts of the island. Liele kept in touch by occasional visits for the purpose of keeping things in proper order. The most important of these schools was in Spanish Town" the capital of Jamaica.[108] Some of Liele's church schools not only taught the three R's to all students but also history and grammar to the more advanced students.[109]

Liele's church schools did not reserve education for a particular class or caste or color. In his schools the children of slaves and freedmen were received. Reserving certain educational opportunities based on social or caste status was an insidious idea that came into existence much later in Jamaican history. Prime Minister Norman Manley, in the 1970s, articulated a nationwide effort to teach ever person in Jamaica to read, thereby banishing illiteracy from the island.

The formula George Liele had initiated for years, using Baptist chapels and buildings to educate slave and free children, must have amazed the British missionaries. Church school had been a novel, even controversial, church development in England. We can only speculate as to how a slave preacher in an English colony was introduced to and became an advocate of Christian education. Only two years before George Liele reached Jamaica, in 1780, an Evangelical English layman, the publisher of the *Gloucester Journal* named Robert Raikes, initiated the first systematic and successful effort to reach the poor and unschooled in England. Using paid teachers, Raikes provided Christian training on Sundays, the only day children as young as ten years of age who were working fourteen to sixteen hours a day and dying from lung related diseases in clothing factories and coal mines could attend. Since the schools were free, the only requirement was that the children also attend church. They were taught reading and arithmetic as well as Bible knowledge. In spite of opposition from the clergy of Anglican Churches, the Sunday Church School idea was immediately favored by the founder of Methodism, John Wesley, and other Non-Conformist groups including the English Baptists.

When the British arrived in Jamaica with instructions from the directors of the British Missionary Society to build upon and expand on the foundations already in place by Liele and Baker, they did so with fervor and zeal. One of the most honored British missionaries and proponents of mass education was the Reverend James Murcell Phillippo. In 1825, he became the pastor of the Baptist church in Spanish Town that had been organized by George Liele seven years earlier.

Phillippo discovered, as did other Baptist missionaries, that by closing all slave churches in 1806 and prohibiting slave preachers such as Liele to conduct services or meetings, especially in towns and cities, a state of intellectual torpor had developed among the slaves. With school doors closed, their hope of learning to read was dead. The planters and magistrates not only believed that God was white but they were also convinced that providing the Christian gospel and education to slaves would "revolutionize" the country. Initially, most of the non-Baptist missionaries acquiesced with that anti-education judgement. But the British began an educational initiative to reopen slave churches to children, and their leadership encouraged Wesleyan Methodists and Moravians to reconsider their positions.[110] Adult slaves learned to read their Bibles from their children. In a short period of time, the spelling book became a powerful factor of Christian enlightenment. Through mission schools thousands were brought under the direct influence of the Gospel.[111]

The efforts of the Reverend Phillippo were exceptional. The First Baptist Church of Spanish Town built schools for the children of both free and enslaved. In addition, a "School of Industry" was created for poor children who were not able to make it in academic classrooms. Other Baptist missionaries, such as William Knibb, the brother of Thomas Knibb, were just as zealous, establishing schools for blacks throughout Jamaica. William Knibb, as soon as he arrived in Jamaica, placed an advertisement in the local newspaper, seeking students but notably taking care not to offend the plantocracy by announcing that "slave children must be brought by their owners or accompanied with a note from them."[112] Years later, after emancipation was realized and Jamaica became a crown colony, the Reverend Phillippo was asked to design a system of elementary education (a chapel and a school on every plantation) which was financed by government grants.[113] When the Jamaican legislature repealed laws prohibiting blacks to preach or teach, several resolutions to train Afro-Jamaicans were passed by a group of mostly orthodox Jamaican Baptist pastors who formed an organization known as the Jamaica Baptist Missionary Society (JBMS). Three years later, in 1842, with the enthusiastic support of Missionary pastors Phillippo, Thomas Burchell and Knibb, the JBMS requested the British Missionary Society to fund such a school to enhance Christian ministry among the Afro-Jamaicans.

Calabar College opened as a theological school in 1843, located at Rio Bueno, Trelawny not far from Montego Bay. The coastal village in West Africa for which the college was named, had been an African depot in Benin (Nigeria) during the Atlantic Slave Trade from which slaves were shipped directly to Jamaica. The schools first superintendent was a British missionary, Joshua Tinson, who was serving as the pastor of East Queen Street Baptist Church in Kingston. He earned money to support himself by working a little as a mechanic.[114] Incidently, many of the founding members of East Queen Street had originally been members of Windward Road Baptist Chapel organized by the pioneer Baptist, George Liele.

Calabar did not begin with resounding success. The first ten students, all older men who were dedicated but mostly illiterate, eventually dropped out, although all of them acquired some skills in reading, composition and pronunciation as well as rudiments of Hebrew and Greek. British missionary attempts to train Afro-Jamaican ministers to supply new mission churches and replace them at others, failed. Phillip Curtin suggests several factors which were responsible for the low number and quality of students and their decision to leave. One factor, according to Philip Curtin, was the loss of Afro-Jamaicans as members of churches with British Missionary leadership as pastors. The blacks resented British missionary attempts to consider and promote themselves as the leaders of the Afro-Jamaican communities in things religious, moral and cultural. For one thing, many blacks considered their morals, dancing, drumming, concubinage, the Christmas festival, and Sabbath breaking as private and privileged concerns separate from their religion. Also, British missionary pastors discouraged baptizing "illegitimate" children (born of parents who were not married or not married to each other). The result was that seventy percent of the Afro-Jamaican population was barred from being members of British missionary or orthodox Afro-Jamaican Baptist Churches like those founded by George Liele. Many young women, especially, considered church approval of their sexual practices and the necessity of legalized marriage as a form of slavery.[115]

The decreasing number of Afro-American Jamaicans as members of missionary-led churches also reflected a growing distrust. That distrust, according to Curtin, contributed to the small number of students enrolled at Calabar College. As time passed, Blacks tended to prefer ministers of their own color who were not under the supervision or control of the missionaries. Afro-Jamaican class leaders, such as George William Gordon, dropped out of British-missionary led churches to form congregations under the independent Native Baptist banner. To be trained as a minister or parson at a British missionary college like Calabar, became a stamp of rejection by the Afro-Jamaican people.[116]

The failure of Calabar College, never well planned or well financed by the British Missionary Society, to train and influence Afro-Jamaicans to prepare for church leadership was one of the factors that gave impetus to the formation of a group of Jamaican Baptist pastors known as the Jamaican Baptist Union, who wanted to become independent of London. Within a few years, Calabar, under Afro-Jamaican control, was enlarged, adding a training school for teachers. In 1869, the buildings were dismantled and reconstructed in Kingston as a part of the East Queen Street Baptist Church.

Early in the twentieth century the colonial Jamaican government undertook the training of school teachers and withdrew grants formerly made to religious denominational colleges forcing Calabar to close. In 1904, a new site in Kingston was selected side by side with a teachers training school and Calabar High School for boys was constructed. It became renown throughout the West Indies as a well-equipped facility with a consistently superior academic record. Calabar College and High School has been one of the most significant contributions made by the British and Afro-Jamaican Baptists to the Christian Church in Jamaica and the West Indies. Today it exists to provide training to young men and women for various professions other than religion and theology. Religious education and theological training for Baptists and other Protestant denominations is now a unified denominational effort at the United Theological College of the West Indies, formed in 1966, located at Mona near the University of West Indies in Kingston.

NOTES

[108]Gayle, p. 22; John Rippon, *The Baptist Annual Register, 1790-1793* (London, n.p.n.d.) P.105.)
[109]Turner, p. 87.
[110]Ibid., p. 86.
[111]Sherlock and Bennett, p. 240.
[112]Lawson, p. 173.
[113]Ibid, p.174; E.B. Underhill, *The Life of James Murcell Phillippo* (London: Jackson, Wolford and Hodden, 1881), pp. 169-70.
[114]Payne, p. 108.
[115]Curtin, Philip, *Two Jamaicas: The Role of Ideas in a Tropical Colony, 1830-1865.* (Westport, CT., Greenwood Press, 1968), p. 169.
[116]Ibid.

Chapter Nine

THE LIELE LEGACY: JAMAICA BAPTIST MISSIONS

Jamaica Baptist Missionary Society

The Jamaica Baptist Missionary Society (JBMS) was organized by British Baptist missionaries serving in Jamaica in 1842. One of the goals, in light of substantial decreased financial aid from the London-based British Missionary Society, was to make the Baptist churches in Jamaica self-sufficient and financially self-supporting. That would lead to diminishing control from London and a state of independence for English Baptists in Jamaica. Of equal importance, the society supported a concern intensely articulated by British and Afro-Jamaican pastors - sending Afro-Jamaican missionaries to West Africa, Haiti, Cuba, and other parts of the Caribbean.[117] Their urgency, especially since Emancipation, was matched by that of the British Missionary Society that had always considered West Africa its primary mission field. As financial and personnel resources earmarked for Jamaica were diverted to West Africa, the Jamaican Baptist Missionary Society, in a desperate attempt to revert to better days, dissolved itself in 1843 and became an independent Jamaican Church rather than a British missionary outpost.

Afro-Jamaican Baptist Foreign Mission Efforts

During the half century of Afro-Jamaican Baptist development, from 1783 to 1834, the fundamental concerns of the leadership and members, slaves and freemen, related to survival. The abolition of slavery, justice, political and economic opportunities for the oppressed black masses overshadowed other concerns. Frequently, English Baptist missionaries were allied to those goals also. It was not until the emancipation of Afro-Jamaicans that their minds were able to focus on decades-old concerns for the spiritual welfare of fellow blacks in West Africa, Haiti and elsewhere in the Caribbean Basin. The need to export the Christian Gospel was shared by one British missionary in particular, the Reverend William Knibb, pastor of the Falmouth Baptist Church, who had been a valiant leader of the Anti-Slavery Society in England.

In 1839, Knibb announced that an Afro- Jamaican named Thomas Keith was already in West Africa. About Keith, who was commissioned by British missionaries in Jamaica the same year David Livingston of Africa missionary fame was born, the Reverend Knibb wrote, "a beloved brother, one of the despised, traduced black Christians, *an Africana by birth* (italics writer) . . . taking with him only a letter of introduction from his late pastor . . . and without any support or countenance, except from God . . . is now on the spot from whence he was stolen when a boy, telling his fellow-countrymen the name of Jesus. . . . He has written one letter which I have seen."[118] Keith's determination and endured hardships to preach the gospel against formidable odds closely parallels that of George Liele. Both arrived on mission fields with only letters of introduction to people they did not know. Both arrived, Liele in Jamaica and Keith in West Africa, without organizational support or sponsorship of any kind.

The glory of it all is that just as George Liele was the first African-American voice to be heard proclaiming the Gospel and Baptist Christianity in Jamaica, Thomas Keith was the first African-Jamaican Baptist Christian preacher in West Africa! The Reverend Lott Carey, the honored African-American missionary, had already reached Cape Montserado and organized a church seventeen years earlier, in 1822.

In the years following, many Afro-Jamaican members of Jamaican Baptist churches, sponsored and supported by both the Jamaican and British Baptist Missionary Societies, served, and died, as missionaries at a minimum of seven locations from north of the Cameroons River all the way south to the Congo in West Africa. About them, the historian Earnest A. Payne wrote the following tribute: "The mission to Africa was a magnificent unforgettable gesture by those who had suffered the curse of slavery. It was perhaps premature, but it is increasingly clear that the real evangelization of Africa will be done by men and women of the African race."[119]

Even as one celebrates the achievements of the Afro-Jamaican Baptists in West Africa, one may also wonder if Thomas Keith and the other missionaries even knew the name of the black Baptist preacher who was responsible for them being Baptist and Christian in the first place. Like thousands in Jamaica today, they probably never understood that, as Afro-Jamaican Baptists, *they were extending a religious cultural gospel thread to West Africa that was Christian and Baptist (italics writer)*. The tread had begun with the inspired vision of a slave named George Liele in a British colony in North America and had been extended from Georgia to Jamaica. Through the Afro-Jamaican Baptists, it had been extended to West Africa, and through others, to Haiti, Trinidad, Barbados and other parts of the Caribbean Basin.

Notes

[117] Gayle, p. 36.
[118] Payne, pp. 73-74.
[119] Ibid., p. 84.

Chapter Ten

THE LIELE LEGACY: BAPTIST FRUIT OF EMANCIPATION

Emancipation and Land Ownership Baptist Style

An act of Emancipation was enacted by the English Parliament and signed by the King on August 28, 1833. It granted emancipation to all slaves in Jamaica and was bestowed in two parts. Part One decreed that while slavery was abolished and all slaves manumitted, they were to become "apprenticed laborers" for a period of four years, from August 1834 to August 1838. During the four years, sugar planters would have time to adjust to the loss of their slave labor force and receive compensation from the British government for the inconvenience and expected financial losses. The only planter to grant immediately full freedom to his slaves was the Marquis of Sligo, the governor appointed by the King to administer the apprenticeship system.

Two churches were designated by the British Missionary pastors in Jamaica as church locations where Jamaican slaves would gather for Emancipation Day Services. One was the church that had grown out of a group of Afro-Jamaicans baptized by George Liele. Later, the group was organized as the First Baptist Church of Spanish Town by a British missionary named Christopher Kitchen. Years later, First Baptist was renamed Phillippo Baptist Church in honor of the freedom loving missionary pastor, James Phillippo.

The other church designated for an Emancipation Day service was the Falmouth Baptist Church in northwest Jamaica, initially organized by George Liele's colleague in ministry, Moses

Baker. On the evening of July 31, 1838, the soon-to-be-free slaves gathered in and outside both churches for all-night prayer and praise meetings. At midnight, in Spanish Town, the British Missionary pastor, James Phillippo, stood and announced, "Freedom has come." The newly free men and women, with voices raised in songs of joy, lit candles and walked and danced out of the church and several blocks to the town square. A hearse containing all of the iron chairs, shackles and pain inflicting instruments of slave punishment, torture and death the people could find, was pulled through the town. When the hearse reached First Baptist Church, former slaves joyously dug a deep hole located to right of the church entrance into which the slaves had the privilege of throwing the emblems of more than three hundred years of their pain, misery and bondage. They wept as the symbols of their sorrow disappeared into the ground. A tamarind tree was planted on that grave site to mark the spot forever. Although gnarled with stunted limbs and branches, the tree still stands.[120] Because the fruit of the tamarind tree is sour, many Jamaicans call the sorrow days of slavery and life in general, tamarind times. On the other hand, emancipation of the slaves and good times in general are called 'mango times' because the fruit of mango tree is sweet and tasty.

In Falmouth, at the Falmouth Baptist Church, the author Earnest A. Payne describes the Emancipation events as follows. The word "Freedom" was printed over the door of the church. At midnight, the British missionary and abolitionist pastor, William Knibb, arose and declared, "The monster is dead, the Negro is free." An iron chain and collar used to punish and torment slaves was buried in a special coffin near the church and the flag of England was raised over the spot.[121]

For many years, especially in Spanish Town and rural communities, Emancipation Day Celebrations continued to have strong religious overtones which included church services, a setup or wake on Emancipation Eve. and a pilgrimage to particular places to recognize the end of slavery in Jamaica. Children and adults marched around their villages and from one village to another, carrying banners to the accompaniment of drums.[122]

Once the euphoria of emancipation was over, the former slaves of Jamaica quickly learned that freedom offered very limited opportunities. "Emancipation gave them the right to free movement, the right to choose where they wished to work, but without basic education and training many were compelled to remain on the plantation...under conditions determined by the . . . (planter) . . . for wages set by him."[123] Baptist missionary pastors provided real assistance and hope. From sympathetic friends of the English Abolition and Missionary societies, British missionaries like the Reverends James Phillippo and William Knibb obtained money to purchase small acreage of land, sometimes from former slave plantation owners. The land was then subdivided into small lots and distributed to newly manumitted Afro-Jamaicans for very reasonable prices. They reimbursed the missionaries with money earned from selling crops, fowl, animals and other garden products. As the loans were repaid, the missionaries used the money to purchase additional land which was also subdivided into plots for other freedmen.

Parenthetically, a history researcher, Richard D.E. Burton, points out that even during the last years of slavery in Jamaica, many slaves considered the houses in which they lived and the provision grounds on which they raised subsistence crops as their own property, even though they were on their owners plantations. It was even common, according to Burton, for huts, gardens, and other possessions to be bequeathed by one slave to another. Cash transactions for goods and services were part of everyday life.[124] It is commonly accepted that many slaves —in Jamaica as well as on other islands in the West Indies—were virtually self-sufficient in food production. Many sold their surplus at Sunday markets throughout the island, as well as buying and selling food, clothes, housewares, tobacco, and luxury items such as jewelry, scarves, and handkerchiefs. It is estimated that as many as ten thousand slaves attended Kingston markets every Sunday. And amazing as it may seem, even planters bought pigs and calves from their slaves, paying them in cash.[125]

The Baptist missionary, James Phillippo, was the first to establish a free village (or township). His planned free village was located in the hill country north of Spanish Town. He named it Sligoville in honor of the Marquis de Sligo, Governor of Jamaica. Other Baptist missionaries concretized their support of new freedmen and their families. Members and friends of the British Missionary Society were heavily involved in the enormous land procurement effort. In all, about 8,000 villages were established in Jamaica permitting approximately 100,000 former slaves to purchase land and establish new settlements like Sligoville.[126]

The missionaries' timely process permitted former slaves to become land owners and farmers, laying the foundation of a peasant class in rural Jamaica. By 1861, Burton estimates that there were 50,000 small proprietors owning an average of three acres each. From the very beginning, Burton contends, "land was (and commonly remains so) "family land" before anything else" never to be sold for any reason. Land became an inheritance for future generations, "reflecting family continuity and identity. . . ."[127]

Women, known as higglers, usually sold the products of the land at the markets. This practice helped to establish the foundation of the entrepreneur spirit that so often characterizes the people of Jamaica and other former British colonies of the West Indies and northern Caribbean area, such as the Bahama Islands.[128] The creation of a subsistence economy for the Afro-Jamaican freed men and women plus the opportunities to become small entrepreneurs comprise the basis of a Jamaican tradition often observed and criticized by African Americans.

George Liele and Moses Baker, had they lived, doubtlessly would have rejoiced to witness the practical Baptist schema to help former slaves, in a holistic way, claim the opportunities their new freedom provided. After all, the Baptist land purchases were directly related to and were another result of their pioneering effort to lift their Afro-Jamaican brothers and sisters. British missionaries were serving in Christian ministry only because of their successful efforts to establish Baptist Christian churches and schools. Their pleas for financial and practical assistance to the English Baptists had born fruit in ways they could never have envisioned. They, Liele and Baker, were the reason the British missionaries were in Jamaica as well as Africa, Burma and India.

Other Significant Areas of British Missionary Activity

Immediately after Emancipation Day, in 1838, British Missionary pastors became strongly involved in the former slaves fight to maintain their 'claims' to the land and the development of a growing peasantry. They also championed the freedmen's need to resolve problems related to wages, hours of work and rent of houses. Protest meetings were organized that not only provided forums for expressions of hope and desires for the future, but taught the freedmen how to respond collectively to unfair planter practices, to protest colonial legislation, to petition the colonial authorities and to organize nonviolent strikes and campaigns for resolving their concerns. As a result, the manumitted plantation workers effectively utilized collective bargaining in the immediate post-emancipation period to gain concessions from plantation owners rather than being forced to use armed resistance, protests and violent confrontation. The planters, land owners and colonial authorities turned their dissatisfaction and anger on the British missionaries.[129]

Baptist Missionary pastors, recognizing that political power was necessary to confront the intransigent power positions of the planters and land owners, were crucial in helping to organize other public meetings to provide a forum for the freedmen's demand for a broader franchise—one that included their participation. Sheller also notes, that beginning in 1839, the freedmen were placing their concerns before the colonial legislature and also "asserting their international solidarity with the continuing anti slavery cause" elsewhere. They were also instructed about how to become knowledgeable about their rights and opportunities to secure land.[130]

A weekly newspaper, *the Baptist Herald and Friend of Africa*, was started in 1839 by Baptist missionaries and published in Falmouth. Its dual assignment was to contribute to the empowerment of the Jamaican freedmen to aid Africans. As a result, the African Missionary Society was organized in Spanish Town. However, the consciousness of being African and of owing some repayment to the people of Africa, was something that Afro-

Jamaicans had felt for many years. As freedmen, they did not wait for clergy leadership. In reality, African missions began with the peasant laity as they become even more expressive of their African identity. That interest especially found a home in the Falmouth Anti-Slavery Society which was formed by former slaves to advance abolition in North America and other parts of the world. Their interest also found support in Native Baptist churches where the focus was always more on the "here-and-now" rather than the "hereafter."[131]

The African-based Myal emphasis on the social, economic and political concerns and conditions of the present world provided greater opportunities for Native Baptist churches to fashion a religious system of their own and still be Christians. They provided opportunities for expedient Afro-Jamaican political mobilization. Some of the British missionary or missionary controlled Afro-Jamaican chapels and prayer houses, where the membership was more Myal than Christian, were seized by Native Baptist leaders. Worship services and prayer meetings of orthodox Baptist churches were disrupted and Myal rites consisting of opening graves and the practice of violent spirit "possessions" were performed publically. Interestingly, the Native Baptist churches exercised self- determination and demonstrated grassroots control. Sheller writes that Native churches even exercised "popular justice," as communities attempted to solve problems including controlling the influence of Obeah men and destroying the evil charms and symbols of sorcerers.[132]

Notes

[120] This description of the night's events is taken from: *The 175th Anniversary Booklet, The Phillippo Baptist Church*, Spanish Town, Jamaica (September 1988), p. 9.
[121] Payne, p. 55.
[122] *Freedom To Be*, p. 61.
[123] Ibid., p. 235
[124] Richard D.E. Burton, *Afro-Creole: Power, Opposition, and Play in*

the Caribbean (Ithaca and London: Cornell University Press, 1997), p. 38.

[125]Ibid.
[126]Sherlock and Bennett, p. 237; Payne, pp. 59-60
[127]Burton, pp. 93-94.
[128]Sherlock and Bennett, p. 170.
[129]Mimi Sheller, *Democracy After Slavery* (Gainesville: University Press of Florida, 2000), pp. 149-150.
[130]Ibid., p. 153.
[131]Ibid., p. 168.
[132]Ibid.

Chapter Eleven

THE LIELE LEGACY: AFRO-JAMAICA BAPTIST LEADERSHIP

The Jamaica Baptist Union

The influence of the Jamaica Baptist Missionary Society began to decline as Native Baptist influence intensified and the British Missionary Society in London heightened its efforts to develop the scope of its missions in other areas of the world, especially West Africa and Asia. Indeed, the Society continued a limited involvement in Calabar College, even though attempts to recruit students there continued to be unsuccessful. The BMS also owned the East Queen Street premises, and had sole legal right to nominate its pastoral leadership. The point has already been made that a decline in the membership of churches led by British missionaries was attributed to the fact that Afro-Jamaicans perceived the British as promoting things religious, moral and cultural. More and more of them began to prefer ministers (or pastors) of their own color who were not under the control of missionary pastors.

The decline, and then dissolution, of the British Missionary led Jamaica Baptist Missionary Society contributed to the organization of the Jamaica Baptist Union made up of orthodox (Non-Native Baptist) congregations that may have at one time been led by British Missionaries or had been organized by George Liele. Promoting self extension, self-supporting and self-governing, the Union became the largest Baptist group (in terms of number of churches and members) in Jamaica. By 1890, it had an aggregate membership of approximately 34,000.[133]

Since 1890, Jamaica Baptist Union churches have undergone periods of growth and decline in membership, quality of pastoral leadership and national influence. The periods of decline have reflected the insincerity of many who professed to be converted Baptists, a conversion not substantiated because of polygamous marital arrangements. When their ministers (pastors) failed, or were unable, to discipline them, many simply joined Native Baptist Churches.[134] Indeed, the Union has continued to be besieged with faith and belief problems associated with the continual attraction of Neo-African religious groups such as obeah and modified Myalism. Religious practices such as Convince, Pukumina (Pocomania) and Revival Zion flourish among the poor and uneducated in the rural areas of Jamaica and the more heavily populated cities of Kingston and Montego Bay. In some instances, traditional church life (Baptist, Methodist and other historic mainline denominations) continues to be challenged by the services and practices of Obeah groups which blend Christianity with Myal ritual and beliefs. These unorthodox groups strongly influence Jamaican family life. It is estimated that in the first half of the twentieth century, about seventy percent of all Jamaican births were from relationships not sanctioned by orthodox Christians which the members of Jamaica Baptist Union churches are supposed to be.[135]

Two additional concerns have also affected the decline in membership and influence of the Jamaica Baptist Union churches. In its early years, writes Stanley, financial problems consumed the JBU, a condition that undoubtedly reflected the impoverished conditions of the members of its churches. Initially, the Baptists in Jamaica were landless "day labourers . . . who had 'practically no money most of their time.'"[136] Associated with the problems of money was the lack of pastoral leadership. English missionary church leaders decreased. The failure of the British Missionary pastors to recruit students for Baptist church leadership at Calabar College has already been discussed. By 1904, there were only sixty-three pastors for 202 Jamaica Baptist Union related churches. Seventeen years later (1921) some pastors were responsible for as many as six churches and pastoral care was replaced (reverting to the initial years of the Baptist pioneer, George Liele) by deacons and class leaders, many of whom by that time were women. Most of them were without formal biblical and theological training but were responsible for the management of church finances since educated, middle-class Baptists were virtually nonexistent. Many church members only saw their pastors on Communion Sunday. The members responded by being less willing to contribute to sustain a distant minister.[137]

The Jamaica Baptist Union received little, and at times, no financial support from the British Missionary Society. A leading American Baptist layman, Thomas Penney (founder of the J.C. Penney store chain and the Penney Farms Retirement Community Development near Jacksonville, Florida) was instrumental in convincing the directors of the American Baptist Home Society (now the American Baptist Churches, USA.) to consider financial aid to Calabar College. Other grants were given to support individual former British missionary pastors who continued to lead churches in Jamaica. Until the 1980s, the Jamaica Baptist Union continued to look to the BMS and Baptist churches in Canada for assistance in maintaining Baptist representation on the faculty of the United Theological College of the West Indies in Kingston. That institution has assumed the religious and theological teaching responsibilities associated with preparing men and women for Christian ministry which were initially those of Calabar College.[138]

NOTES

[133] Ibid.
[134] Ibid., pp. 241-242.
[135] Simpson, p. 262.
[136] Stanley, p. 242.
[137] Ibid, p. 242.
[138] Ibid., pp. 242, 243, 262.

Chapter Twelve

WHAT CHURCH DENOMINATION SPEAKS FOR THE JAMAICAN MASSES?

The Growth of Non-Historic Church Groups

The years of the declining effectiveness of churches associated with the Jamaica Baptist Union produced the rapid expansion of relatively new Christian denominations. The growth of these groups is also evident throughout the West Indies Basin. A statement that Simpson attributes to a mainline Protestant pastor in 1941, who was commenting on their twenty-five years of rapid growth in Jamaica, seems to have been prophetic. "Our sober and unemotional type of service cannot compete with the drumming, dancing, and emotionalism of these sects."[139] For many years, so-called Orthodox church groups such as the Baptists refused to consider the new Christian groups threatening, and therefore, unworthy of being taken seriously.

Orthodox Jamaican Baptists (other than Native Baptists) have accepted many class status assumptions held by other Protestant Church leaders. For the most part, they disdainfully noted street revivals and crowds attending street type services of the newer "sects" at bus depots and in parks and assumed that it was a dangerous phenomenon, sub-Christian in theology and ethic. They wrongly assumed that what they were witnessing was indicative of a temporary and passing movement that would die out or undergo modification within traditional (historic) Protestantism.[140]

The Church of God and Pentecostalism

In 1941, a Protestant pastor commented that the new forms of religion had grown rapidly in the twenty-five previous years in Jamaica, and added "Our sober and unemotional services cannot compete with the drumming, dancing, and emotionalism of these sects."[141] In 1955, the president of Union Theological Seminary (New York City) reported that he was surprised and impressed by the rapid growth of the "fringe sects" such as Pentecostal, Adventist, Holiness, Church of God and Church of Christ. The term 'sect' or 'fringe sects' refers to what J. Milton Yinger, has called "a religious protest against a system in which attention to the various individual functions of religion has been obscured and made ineffective by the extreme emphasis on social and ecclesiastical order."[142]

The statistics of membership show that the Church of God grew from 1,777 in 1921 to 340,000 in 1970 becoming, at that time, the second largest religious group and seventeen percent of the Jamaican population. All Baptist churches combined had a membership representing eighteen percent. In 1982, the Church of God, according to official census figures, consisted of over 400,000.[143] The conclusion is that the Baptist denomination no longer appeals to the majority of Jamaicans and does not speak for the lower class poor and illiterate.

Other Christian Groups or Sects

Richard D.E. Burton, in his sobering analysis of religious leadership as it impacts on the social and political power and economic opportunity for the West Indian masses, concluded that in the decades following the Morant Bay uprising of the newly emancipated masses, colonial leaders formed an alliance with Anglican church and educational leaders. Furthermore, Burton argued, the aim of that alliance was to curb the kind of religious by-products to which the Afro-Jamaican masses were being subjected. Similar efforts had been made by the mainline churches such as

Methodists, Presbyterians, Moravians and Baptists (churches led by British and foreign missionaries or Afro-Jamaicans trained by them) to strengthen their hold on the existing colored (Creole) middle-class and the emerging black lower class who remained outside their circle of influence.[144] Burton also correctly recognized that the black lower class not only participated in new Christian sect-groups, but also in a variety of Neo-African-Christian groups ranging from Native Baptist churches to the Convince cult, Afro-Christian Pocomania and Revival Zion. Many of those 'religions' were apocalyptic, depicting symbolically the ultimate destruction of evil and triumph, urging members to live strict moral lives based on faith group associations. Other groups, usually presented as diabolic, were to be shunned completely.[145]

Bedwardism (a.k.a. the Bedwardian Revival)

Sometimes called the Bewardian Revival, Bedwardism was a movement that combined religious and political agendas. In 1891, Alexander Bedward who had been a member of the H.E. Shakespeare Wood's Native Free Baptist Church in August Town near Kingston, began to preach a radical form of Myal and Christianity that included baptism by immersion and healing services. More than a spontaneous outburst, it was a formal church. His messages, couched in religious terminology and imagery, were theologically based on a strong, orthodox, Christian New Testament consciousness, especially with regard to the emphasis on the Trinity, the Christian term for the community of God as three divine "Persons" (Father, Son, and Holy Spirit). At the same time, his sermons were directed at social and political concerns that focused on two walls, one white that oppressed black Jamaicans for years, the other black. Since the black wall had become the biggest, it was time, according to Alexander Bedward, to knock the white wall down.

Patrick Bryan, a lecturer at the University of the West Indies, points out that while the Bedwardian Revival was one of the most vigorous in Jamaican history, it was disapproved by the Jamaican upper and middle classes because they shared a dislike for and feared Afro-Jamaican religious expression. Bryan believes that the Bewardian Revival, like others, suggests "that the Churches of Jamaica had, by the 1880s, lost some of the evangelical vitality of the earlier decades."[146] Bedwardism, however, strongly appealed to the rural and urban lower-class poor people. It is considered the link between Morant Bay protest, preparing the way for the more contemporary group known as Rastafarians.[147] Bedward died in November 1930, a few weeks after the coronation of Emperor Haile Selassie I of Ethiopia.

Rastafarianism and Pentecostalism: A Challenge to Jamaican Baptists Identity

Leonard Perceval Howell, one of the several preacher-leaders who started the Rastafarian movement, believed that Marcus Garvey, the founder of the Universal Negro Improvement Association (UNIA) was a prophet, a Biblical John the Baptist incarnate. Garvey's messages promoting his Back To Africa movement galvanized thousands of African-Americans in the United States in the early twentieth century and set the stage for Rastafarianism in Jamaica. When Howell was a migrant working in the United States, he had encountered Garvey, and Africa. When he returned from Africa after fighting in the Ashanti War of 1896, able to speak several African languages, he began his ministry among the Jamaican lower-class black masses in the slums of West Kingston. His messages declared Haile Selassie, whom he called "Ras" (a title) "Tafari" (Selassie's family name), Emperor of Ethiopia, and presented him as the Supreme Being and the only ruler of black people, their new king.[148] On the strength of that belief, Africa, for the Rastafarians (also Rastas), was always at the center of Jamaican concerns.

Three factors contributed to the rise of the Ratafarian movement. First, the movement offered the more radical and displaced males of Jamaican society a needed contemporary movement for protest and self-affirmation, something that had been offered earlier by the eighteenth century Baptists and Native Baptist church movement. Second, historical Baptists, whose pastors were associated with the Jamaica Baptist Union, sometimes still strongly influenced by the British, had become a haven for middle-class Afro-Jamaicans. A perceptible moderation of the early Baptist social message was frequently heard from those pulpits. Like other mainline denominations, the orthodox Baptists fostered the social, political and spiritual values of the Jamaican middle-class. Many Baptist pastors and church leaders, like other upper-class Jamaicans, having been exposed to educational advantages such as secondary schools and graduate study in foreign countries, especially in England and Canada, looked on the working class with disdain. A few pastors of major urban churches entered the political arena and were elected to serve in the Jamaican parliament, sometimes its House of Lords, historically the citadel of the rich land-owners and socially privileged.

The third factor contributing to the development of the Rastafarian movement was the emergence of Pentecostalism as the dominant religion of poor Jamaicans, especially working women. This church group has been described by Richard D. E. Burton as a "mass form of supportive psychotherapy for casualties of the modernization process. Lower-class women in that setting, at least in Jamaica, derived companionship, not only with a personal Jesus, but also with women like themselves through belonging to a close-knit and usually small-scale, locally based church community."[149] Politically, Pentecostalism offered its members a moral order in which issues of race and other social concerns (were) neutralized as members were encouraged to strive for holy living. It was not surprising that they became a very conservative force. For a while, as in most church groups, the leaders of Pentecostal churches in Jamaica were men. However, as women became more educationally qualified than black men, they soon dominated, and perhaps still dominate their churches, not only in membership numbers, but also in occupying the intermediate positions between the leadership and the generality of worshipers who were predominantly females.[150]

Interestingly, as "respectable" lower-class women flocked to Pentecostal churches, thousands of young lower-class males, left outside the fold of Christianity in both its orthodox mainstream and Pentecostal type churches, were easily enticed by Rastafarianism that provided both a religion with a male African deity and an unorthodox political agenda. Yoshiko S. Nagashima contends that young black males seem to have withdrawn from Baptist and Methodist churches to follow the pre-Rastafarian, Alexander Bedward, because of his provocative and appealing racial messages which were full of mysticism and prophecy.[151]

Rastafarianism is a religious-political system of contradictions. As Burton points out, it totally rejects Christianity but has originated no sacred scripture of its own. It uses the Christian Bible by verbally manipulating various texts or verses in such a way that the authority of the Bible is retained and black-white polarization is reversed. Smoking "the herb" (ganja) is raised to the level of a religious sacrament.[152] Rastafarian men proclaimed their identify by wearing dreadlocks, formerly a mark of femininity, to set themselves apart from the English "world of Babylon" which Jamaicans had embraced, and most of all, from the world of women. Among the Rastas, women are subordinated in the movement and the matrifocal household is rejected as a product of slavery. Instead, Rasta men emphasize father-centered family structures in the name of "Africa," ironically duplicating Jamaican middle-class family life values. The internationally acclaimed Rastafarian dreadlock promoter of Reggae music, Bob Marley, is supposed to have told an interviewer, "Woman is a coward, man strong." Some Rastawomen repeat, "the dread is the head."[153]

The reformist Dreadlocks (as they are sometimes called) oppose religious cults such as Revival and Pentecostal-type churches as expressions of "female" passivity. And yet, as Burton observes, it is their strong desire to purge Rastafarianism ritual of any Revivalist taint that may have brought it back toward Christianity, and specifically nonconformist Protestant (Native Baptist) practice. Their emphasis on scriptural exegesis and "reasoning" while rejecting possession by the Spirit or spirits is precisely what George Liele, British missionaries and orthodox Baptist preachers have proclaimed since 1783. One wonders, could this fact be one "ray of hope" for Baptists survival and growth in Jamaica?

As a second generation modified "orthodox" Baptist who has grave concerns about the survival of Baptist churches in Jamaica and the United States, the writer wonders what might happen if young Jamaicans who are members of Baptist churches today, or whose parents used to be, were given the opportunity to participate in worship services that promote contemporary Christian worship, liturgies and even music with a non-traditional drum beat such as that originated by Count Ossie and Reggae rhythm makers. Of course, it is the non-traditional music and worship format that may be causing many older adults great stress. Some are having difficulties adjusting to it and are resisting all changes. Nevertheless, it may be that such worship settings combined with preaching in contemporary language but grounded in a fundamental Christian biblical hermeneutic that is socially inclusive, may be just what is needed to reach and engage our youth and young adults. Such services are being held for youth and young adults in many African American Baptist churches in the United States. As one listens, one hears cries for a church experience that receives and respects them as they are and teaches the Word of God to lead them to higher spiritual ground. After all, the Lord God had to remind His prophet, Elijah, "Yet I have seven thousand in Israel, all the knees which have not bowed unto Baal, and every mouth which hath not kissed him."[154]

Our forefathers, as they struggled to survive in North America, often compared their life journeys as one of being strangers in a weary land. Rastas sang of oppression in exile and a longing for a place to feel at home. In the Christian holistic context, the bible based gospel message combines the call for personal salvation and commitment of the Sermon on the Mount with the challenges and opportunities of service on the Jericho Roads of life. But Rastarianism that began as a socio-religious protest movement became a contemporary entertainment medium. One question, therefore, is whether or not it will become another popular innovation that capitalized on the pain, misery and hopelessness of the lower-class that will become another religious affectation that will fade away or merge into something yet unknown. In fact, Rastafarianism is not now the voice of the Jamaican masses, leading them into a political force that provides hope for the growing number of poor, jobless, uneducated, and untrained.

A second question may be, what contemporary Baptist leaders (or group) will dare to reclaim the heritage of the historic Afro-Jamaican Baptist church movement and organize and empower a "new" contemporary worship and Biblical theological model that transcends lines of class, caste, nationality, gender, race and generation? In a sentence, can Jamaica produce a twenty-first century George Liele or Moses Baker or Sam Sharpe or George Gordon? Or, will the leadership of a Knibb or Phillippo come from another country, perhaps a second or third generation Jamaican who has been liberated from the liabilities of Jamaican class and caste by an education and social maturation in America that has been sharpened by twentieth century black Evangelical religious exposure?

Summary Thoughts

For many years, religion remained at the center of Jamaican national life. Church and school, parson and teacher, worked (and fought) with conservative mainline church leaders and authoritarian and racist government leaders to build into the social fabric a tradition of democratic self-government that honored justice and equality for all. The words of the Right Honorable Edward Seaga, P.C., M.P., a recent unsuccessful candidate for the high office of Prime Minister of Jamaica, wrote a statement that appeared in the 175th Anniversary Booklet of the Phillippo Baptist Church in Spanish Town. To the members of the church named in honor of a British Baptist Missionary who came to Jamaica in response to the invitation of a pioneer Baptist missionary named George Liele, Seaga wrote, "The Baptists were the first religious denomination to reach out to the Jamaican people in a meaningful way when the transition was being made from slavery to freedom. Before any government of Jamaica developed the concept of land settlement, the Baptists established villages in which to settle 20,000 families. Before any government took responsibility for public education, the Baptists set up schools in connection with their churches. The Baptists were the pioneers in political organization and had, by 1844, an organization to procure the election of assembly men who were sympathetic to the newly freed people. This was the first holistic approach to the spread of the gospel."[155] Interestingly, Seaga is not now nor has he ever been a member of a Baptist church.

George Liele's letters which were published by the Reverend John Rippon in his *Baptist Register*, have established proof of positive cooperative support from the British Missionary Society for many years. Because of his exposure in *The Baptist Register*, Liele's contributions to the worldwide fellowship of Baptists all over the British colonies should not be underestimated or forgotten. Even though he may be unknown by most Baptists or forgotten by others, he was the most notable Baptist personage of the late eighteenth and nineteenth century.

Liele brought the Christian religious cultural gospel thread to Jamaica from a British colony in North America called New Georgia. British missionaries and Afro-Jamaican Baptist successors extended that thread to West Africa and Haiti. Prince Williams, another slave preacher, also from British colonial America, extended that thread to the Bahama Islands.

NOTES

[139] Simpson, p. 46.
[140] Ibid., p. 48.
[141] Ibid., p. 46.
[142] Ibid., p. 13.
[143] Ibid., p. 48.
[144] Burton, p.115.
[145] Ibid., p. 114.
[146] Patrick Bryan, *The Jamaican People, 1880-1902, Race, Class and*

Social Control (Jamaica: The University of West Indies Press, 2000), pp. 41-42.

[147]Ibid., p. 143.

[148]Sherlock and Bennett, p. 396; Burton, pp. 123, 125.

[149]Burton, p. 120.

[150]Ibid.

[151]Yoshiko S. Nagashima, *Rastafarian Music In Contemporary Jamaica* (Tokyo: Institute For The Study of Languages and Cultures in Asia and Africa, 1984), p. 36.

[152]Burton, p. 133.

[153]Ibid., pp. 137, 136.

[154]1 Kings 19:19 (KJV)

[155]Phillippo Baptist Church Anniversry Booklet (Spanish Town): 1993, p. 3.

PART II
Baptists in the Bahama Islands

Chapter Thirteen

PIONEER BLACK PREACHERS IN THE BAHAMA ISLANDS

Frank Spence and Prince Williams

The invisible but undeniably religious-cultural gospel thread of Christianity that connects the descendants of African people living in British North America was extended further to the Bahama Islands by the pioneering efforts of men like Frank Spence and Prince Williams. Both were born as slaves on farms in the Long Island area of the English colony of New York and are recognized by many Bahamians as the first African Baptists to proclaim the Christian gospel in their native islands. Little is known of their early lives. Both may have been exposed to what Kenneth Estelle calls, "a type of African spirituality that had taken root in North America . . . (that) . . . merged elements from many African cultures . . .," the result of slave traders intentionally mixing their cargoes of black humanity from many African sources before selling them throughout the North American colonies.[156] The mixing process insured that in no area of North America would a strong or "pure" African culture emerge with a language or religious tradition intact. Of course, as has been noted in Part I, West African traditions of "call and response" in the music and forms of worship in (black) churches that do not have fixed liturgical structure have been retained.

The reader is reminded that for over a century, from 1619 to 1740, the European colonists in North America were fairly indifferent and even hostile to the thought of exposing Africans to Christianity. The general consensus seems to have been that if slaves were baptized and granted church membership, they might begin to consider themselves equal to their white masters in every way. Also, the whites may have reasoned, if slaves became Christians, and were not granted freedom and equality, they might be inspired to rise up in protest and violence. And so, in the northern English colonies, as in the south, for many years slaves spent Sundays in idleness or assembling for dancing, forms of merriment or burying their dead. In 1712, for example, slaves in New York City were all buried on Sundays "in the Common" (a public burial ground) with African, or what the whites called "heathen" rites.[157]

However, as has been noted, as a result of the Evangelical movement in North America known as the Great Awakening (1742 to 1770) a favorable climate for claiming blacks for Christian commitment developed in the northern colonies. Baptists and Methodists (especially Bishop Francis Asbury who frequently traveled with a free black known as Black Harry) were not hostile to the emotionalism of slaves and free blacks who were attracted in large numbers. In fact, the emotion filled services of George Whitfield and John Wesley provided a "festive dimension of slave worship . . . enhanced and encouraged when permission was granted by some slave holders for separate services. . . . (This) provided another opportunity for fellowship and excitement."[158]

Even so, as Melva Costen points out, most of the slave converts may not have committed themselves to attend faithfully worship services only with the people who owned them. Because slaves in the north were often permitted to worship without whites being present, they sought their own worship experiences where their mobility and worship involvement as slaves or free persons may have varied from one community to another. They merged what they understood to be newly learned Christian beliefs and practices with long held traditional (African) symbols, symbolisms and manner of expressions not bound by predetermined models. Instead, worship liturgy for them was constantly evolving as their status changed. Worship based on their own heritage as Africans determined its own limits and boundaries for ritual. Their existential needs were funneled into their living "on the margin" of their reality as slaves or newly freed persons.[159]

Pioneer Preachers in Paradise

The unauthorized preaching of Prince Williams, Frank Spence and other slaves in the Long Island area who probably had only been introduced recently to Christianity were probably the concern of the Anglican minister, D. W. Rose, when he reported to the London-based Society of the Gospel in Foreign Parts in February 1799, that "preachers, black men" had been identified in the New York area as "the followers of St. John . . . misled by strange doctrines . . . artful and designing, making a merchandise of Religion . . . At certain times in the year, . . . Negroes drive numbers into the sea and dip them by way of baptism' for which they extorted a dollar or stolen goods."[160] No historical data of any kind has surfaced so far that suggests that either Williams or Spence were literate, Biblically trained or exposed to either to the Bible or Baptist doctrine by an ordained white Christian minister such as George Liele received in colonial Georgia. Therefore, neither had been licensed or formally ordained by a reputable minister's association. Nevertheless, both men had a zeal and passion that would not diminish to expose other black brethren in bondage to Christianity as they understood it.

Both Prince Williams and George Spence sought refuge from slavery under conditions promised by the British government that guaranteed freedom if they pledged to be loyal to England. Under that umbrella, they opted to leave the New York area and travel to the English controlled city of Charleston in the southern Carolina colony. Once in Charleston, via the slave "grapevine," they heard about the Spanish-controlled city in East Florida called St. Augustine. Although Spanish East Florida may be just a forgotten footnote of history to most Americans, it is important that African-Americans and Baptists understand what opportunities were available to fugitive and free blacks in St. Augustine and the area a few miles north.

St. Augustine: City of Refuge and Hope

St. Augustin, as it was known in colonial years, is the oldest city in North America. It was located in the area identified on early political maps as Spanish East Florida. When it was ceded to

Spain, the Royal Proclamation by King George III of England, designated "the land east of Apalachicola up to the St. Mary's River . . . with its capital at St. Augustine."[161] The city was founded by Pedro Menendez Aviles in 1565 even though Juan Ponce de Leon had visited the area a half century earlier. The first African slaves arrived in 1686 when Spanish soldiers attacked British held Port Royal and Edisto in Jamaica. Among the spoils of war were thirteen Africans. One African was named "Doctor," suggesting that he may have had recognized healing skills. Another was named "Sambo" which comes from an African Hausa tribal word meaning "second son." In the Mends or Val dialect it means "disgrace." The next year, 1687, "the first recorded fugitive slaves" arrived from the English colony north of East Florida known as Carolina. . . . Governor Diego De Carriage dutifully reported to Spain that "eight men, two women and a three-year-old nursing child had escaped to his province in a boat (or canoe). . . ."[162] Jane Landers also reports that the Governor ordered all captured, escaped or runaway slaves who requested instructed in Roman Catholic doctrine to be baptized (and married, if needed). They were then housed in the homes of the Spanish townspeople. He also put the male fugitives to work as iron-smiths and laborers on the new stone fort called the Castillo de San Marcos, the oldest masonry fort in North America for many years and the most northern point of New Spain's territory.[163]

Six years later (1693), Charles II, King of Spain, issued the first official position on runaways and fugitives, a royal edict decreeing that all runaway slaves, men and women, were to be given sanctuary in his (Spanish) colonies. His intent was to set a Spanish example of liberality that the English, French, Dutch would be compelled to emulate.[164] Somehow, the information that all slaves accepting Christianity as Roman Catholics were guaranteed protection as Spanish subjects spread throughout the slave populations of the southern English North American colonies. Of course, the number of slave escapees to Florida steadily increased until, as Dagan and McMahon point out, they probably made up about three percent of St. Augustine's population. "Battling slave catchers, hunger and dangerous swamps, they (the slaves) created the first American underground railroad, more than a century before the Civil War."[165] All blacks who successfully reached St. Augustine immediately became Roman Catholics and Spanish subjects. The men joined the Spanish militia, and in the years that followed, fought valiantly against the British, and later the Americans, when they attacked Spanish settlements in Florida. Except for a period of about ten years (1729 to 1737) St. Augustine remained a city of hope. Governor Manuel de Montiano, in 1737, granted unconditional freedom to all who petitioned for it and abolished the slave market.[166] The policy of religious sanctuary was subsequently extended to other Spanish areas in the Caribbean.

Garcia Real de Santa Teresa de Mose and Fort Mose

Governor Montiano, in 1738, also established the first settlement for free blacks in the New World (including the United States). It was called Gracia Real de Santa Teresa de Mose. According to Landers, the name is a composite of an existing Indian place, Mose. Gracia Real indicated that the new settlement was established by the king. Teresa was the name of the settlement's patron saint, Teresa of Aviles, the patron saint of Spain.[167] It was built on an island along Mose Creek (now Robinson Creek) a tributary of the North River located near the settlement. The settlement not only provided a home for the former slaves but also served as an advance warning system for the city of St. Augustine.

The Governor ordered the black militia to build a fort for the defense of the settlement and augment and strengthen Spanish defenses around the city. He was shrewd enough to understand that the blacks would fight desperately for their freedom and in the process serve the cause responsible for governing the settlement and the fort. Both the settlement and the fort were only in existence for about twenty years.[168] They were captured by English troops and largely destroyed, although Fort Mose was rebuilt and remained in operation until 1763, when Spain, in accordance with a condition of the Treaty of Paris, ceded Florida to England.

At that time all Spanish residents were evacuated to Cuba. According to Landers, "The people of Mose left behind their meager homes and belongings and followed their hosts into exile to become homesteaders in Matanzas, Cuba . . . (located east of Havana) . . . Some . . . eventually relocated to Havana, which offered at least the possibility of a better life, and this last diaspora scattered the black community of Mose."[169] Sometime in the future, according to plans of the black community of St. Augustine, Fort Mose will be rebuilt as a historical landmark under the auspices of the Fort Mose Historical Society. It will be located very close to the original site, just north of St. Augustine city limits east of U.S. Highway A1A.

Even after the Spaniards departed, during and after the Revolutionary War (or War of Independence), St. Augustine under English jurisdiction remained a haven for British Loyalists, freedmen and escaped slaves from other eastern colonial areas from as far north as Boston and New York. For many blacks, the town was often only a stop on a journey to join others who wanted to emigrate to the Bahama Islands, Jamaica and even Nova Scotia. The names of those who emigrated were carefully listed in a certified registrar called, "The Book of Negroes." Only after the Civil War, when England was forced to exchange East Florida for the Bahama Islands, was the door to freedom closed.[170] Prince Williams and Frank Spence were among the hundreds of former slaves and freedmen who emigrated to the Bahama Islands from St. Augustine, East Florida

Notes

[156]Kenneth Estelle, *African American Worship* (Detroit: Visible Ink Press, 1994), pp. 224-225.

[157]Alfred L. Pugh, *African Religions in the West Indies and the United States* (An unpublished manuscript, 1997), pp. 44-45.

[158]Ibid.

[159]Melva Costen, *African American Christian Worship* (Nashville: Abington Press, 1993), pp. 36-37.

[160] Michael C. Symonette and Antonia Canzoneri, *Baptists in the Bahamas* (El Paso: Baptist Spanish Publication House, 1979), pp. 1-2.

[161] Sandra Riley, *Homeward Bound* (Miami: Island Research, 1983), p. 128.

[162] Jane Landers, *Fort Mose, Gracia Real de Santa Tersa de Mose: A Free Black Town in Spanish Florida* (Gainesville: St. Augustine Historical Society, 1992), p. 10.

[163] Ibid.

[164] Ibid., p. 11.

[165] Kathleen Deagan and Darcie MacMahon, *Fort Mose* (Gainesville: University Press of Florida, 1995), p. 19.

[166] A replica of the slave marketplace is located at the east end of the Plaza de la Constitution across from the Bridge of Lions in present day "Old City" St. Augustine.

[167] Landers, p. 15.

[168] Ibid., pp. 15, 16, 32-33.

[169] Landers, pp. 32-33.

[170] Wilmore, p. 248.

Chapter Fourteen

THE BAHAMA ISLANDS BEFORE PRINCE WILLIAMS

The Settlement Process

The settlement process by which the Bahama Islands were populated was substantially different from the way it happened in Jamaica, Haiti and most other islands in the Caribbean West Indies. As in Haiti, the Spaniards, following Christopher Columbus, were responsible for decimating the native (Arawak) population in the Bahama Islands either by killing them or exposing them to diseases such as measles and chickenpox. Arawaks who survived diseases were sent to Cuba or Hispaniola (now the Dominican Republic and Haiti) to be used as slave labor in gold mines and sugar mills. Not until 1648 did a group of English merchants and others from the English colonial island of Bermuda attempt to establish a settlement on a Bahamian island they called Eluthera. Other settlers arrived from eastern colonial port cities such as Boston and Bedford (Massachusetts), New York, Charleston and Savannah. They hoped Eluthera would be the first republic in the New World. However, only after bases that had been used for years by sea pirates were captured and destroyed were permanent settlements possible.

The first census (1731) reported that there were 935 English inhabitants and 453 blacks, probably slaves, living on three of the Bahama Islands known as Eluthera, New Providence and Harbour. The remaining 697 islands were uninhabited.[171] Attempts to cultivate sugar, rice and cotton on plantations similar to those in Jamaica and other colonies in the Caribbean and North America, were unsuccessful. Poor soil quality and severe storms and hurricanes that constantly swept the islands, devastating crops and buildings, were some of the reasons importing slaves directly or indirectly from Africa or other colonies was never established. The slave population on all of the Bahama Islands never exceeded 10,000.[172]

Throughout the ensuing years, the largest number of people settling in the Bahama Islands were refugees including Loyalists, many with slaves even though the English authorities discouraged that policy, and free blacks. The white Loyalists came to escape the harassment of the radical revolutionary element in the North American colonies; free blacks were loyal to England because their non-slave status was guaranteed.[173] Some of the blacks may also have been exposed to unorthodox or modified forms of Christianity. There were also blacks who may have been exposed to Protestant Baptist, Methodist or Presbyterian missionaries after the mid-1700s Great Awakening Revival period and may have become Christians. Whatever their Christian exposure, their religious experiences may have been one of the reasons the preaching and teaching of two untrained, unordained black Baptists named Frank Spence and Prince Williams was so well received.

Frank Spence

Information about Frank Spence is based primarily on the limited research of the Reverend Daniel Wilshere, the honored British missionary who served the Afro-Bahamians as a supervising missionary and later as the first Superintendent of the Bahamas Baptist Union. In a lecture delivered in Miami, Florida in November 1920, Wilshere reported that Frank Spence had been a slave on colonial Long Island, east of New York City, whose owner permitted him to work overtime to earn money to purchase his freedom. According to Wilshere, Spence came under the influence of some indigenous Baptist group who were followers of St. John the Baptist and was converted to "Christianity." Accepting the offer of the British government, Spence declared himself a supporter of the English king, permitting him, and his wife who was still a slave, to leave Long Island with a group of British Loyalists as the Revolutionary War was ending. The first port was St. Augustine where he arranged to leave his wife with a benevolent family in East Florida. He continued on to Nassau on the island of New Providence, arriving, it is estimated, about 1780. He found work and earned money to purchase his wife's freedom and arranged for her to join him.[174]

With very limited literary skills (no formal education or Biblical training) Spence began to share his religious beliefs with other blacks, slaves and freemen. By 1806, he and his followers were able to purchase land in the Eastern District of Nassau on the south side of Fort Fincastle "in the Southern Suburbs" and eventually erect St. Paul's Chapel. Twenty-eight years later (1834) the Bahamas Blue Book noted that Frank Spence's chapel could seat between nine hundred and one thousand people.[175] Unfortunately, over the course of years, the building does not exist and there is no record of what happened to Frank Spence or the members of the congregation. Except for the brief reference by the Reverend Wilshere, only a few sentences by P. Anthony White, a columnist for a Nassau newspaper, may verify its existence. White noted that Spence "founded Spence's Chapel in an area which was most probably Mason's Addition."[176]

Notes

[171] Curtin, pp. 64, 71.
[172] Ibid., p. 88.
[173] Riley, p. 105.
[174] Sybil Russell-Backford, *Bahamas Baptist Union; Glimpses Of The First Ninety Years (1892-1982)* (Nassau: Bahamas Baptist Union, 1982), pp. 39-40.
[175] Ibid., p. 40.
[176] P. Anthony White, "*The Baptist Came, and the Bahamas was never the same,*" The Punch, Punch Publication, Ltd., October 16, 1998, p.18.

Chapter Fifteen

PRINCE WILLIAMS, HONORED AS PIONEER BAPTIST CHURCH FOUNDER

Opportunity Hindered by Personal Adversity

Prince Williams and a friend named Sharper Morris embarked from St. Augustine, sailing in a southernly direction in a small open boat hoping to reach the Bahama Islands. On or about March 25, 1778, perhaps two years before Frank Spence, Williams, and Morris arrived in Nassau harbor on the Bahamian island of New Providence. Their little boat grounded on the small beach area on which the British Colonial Hilton Nassau Hotel stands today—just north of the intersection of West Bay Street and Blue Hill Road.[177]

Prince Williams immediately began to preach and teach in open air street gatherings near what is now Hospital Lane in a section of Nassau just southwest of Government House, the residence of the Governor of the Bahama Islands. The first black Baptist group, known as the Society of Anabaptists, was formed in 1790 and consisted of Prince Williams and other free blacks. It is considered to be the beginning of the first and oldest "continuing" Baptist congregation in the Bahama Islands. "The first . . . (official) . . . documentation for this group is the deed to property on Meeting Street . . ."(the site of the present Bethel Baptist Church). ". . . purchased on August 10, 1801. . . . It is required by law that five freed men had to sign the deed for the purchase of property by a (religious) society. . . . The trustees signing the deed were Prince Williams (identified as a carpenter), John Williams (brother of Prince Williams), Bristol Scriven (or Sherman), William Rivers, Thomas Reid and Archibald Parker."[178]

Later, although no date is given, a wooden structure was built from Anabaptist Society funds. It may have been the first building of any kind constructed in the undeveloped Delancy Town section of Nassau. It was known as Bethel Baptist Meeting House from which the name Meeting Street was derived. Later, the name was changed to Bethel Baptist Church.[179]

Although the article is not documented, C. Powell, editor of the Bethel Baptist Church Newsletter, noted that the land on which the church was constructed was bequeathed to Prince Williams by one Amos Williams, a man of color, from the English colony of South Carolina.[180] Dr. Walter H. Brooks recorded that the pioneer Baptist pioneer, the Reverend George Liele, in one of his letters, perhaps to John Rippon, mentions a "Brother Amos" as one influenced by him. Liele wrote, "Brother Amos . . . appears to have been a product of the colored church at Silver Bluff, South Carolina. Amid the changes wrought . . . this Negro preacher had his lot cast in New Providence, Bahama Islands, British West Indies. According to Liele, Amos (the Reverend Amos Williams) had a membership of three hundred in 1791 . . . in 1812 . . . the Church at New Providence numbered eight hundred and fifty."[181] Obviously, Brother Amos Williams' transferal of land to Prince Williams was a major factor in the growth of Bethel Baptist Church. The interesting thing about it all is that even in the Bahama Islands, indirectly, the impact and influence of George Liele, the pioneer Baptist preacher, missionary and church founder was evident. Amos Williams, almost an obscure personality of history, extended the invisible gospel thread of Christianity, that originated in colonial British America, to the Bahama Islands. Though unseen, the witness of Christianity by the black Baptist missionary connection is history.

Resuming the story of Prince Williams, in spite of his vision and obvious dynamic leadership, when the meeting house was completed, according to Symonette and Canzoneri, "Samba Shriven was elected Pastor and Prince Williams became the Assistant Pastor."[182] One wonders if Sambo Shriven, also mentioned in the 2002 *Bethel's Willing Workers Newsletter*, may not have been the Bristol Skervan (a.k.a. Scriven) whose name

Bethel Baptist Church, Nassau.

appears on the deed for the land on which the building was erected.[183] Nevertheless, the man remembered as Sambo Scriven was elected as Pastor of the congregation rather than Prince Williams. Symonette and Canzoneri suggest that his election may have been due to the fact that the membership was aware that Williams had never formally married the woman he had been living with after purchasing her freedom. He seems to have spent seven years, from 1815 to 1822, on Harbour Island to discontinue their relationship. The members of the church were probably informed that to elect Prince Williams as pastor would have been illegal since the laws of the colonial legislature and the Anglican Church stated that no one could even be accepted as a members of a church or "society" if he or she was living with someone without the benefit of marriage. In 1835, the Attorney General of the Bahama Islands declared, "all marriages performed by a clergyman (meaning British Baptist or Methodist) between slaves and free blacks to be invalid." Not until 1839 were ministers of all denominations, regardless of race and social standing, given permission to perform marriages in the Bahama Islands, and then, only as long as they were set aside (licensed and ordained) to ministry by some known (and approved) sect, church or society.[184]

Just before the Reverend Scriven died in 1822, Prince Williams returned to Nassau without common-law companionship. The majority of the members chose him as the second pastor of Bethel Baptist Church. Williams, however, requested that the members permit him to have an unmarried female housekeeper, which was approved. Nevertheless, his pastoral relationship at Bethel lasted for only three years.

The Bahamas colonial legislature, dominated by the Anglican Church, in December 1816, enacted a law requiring all Methodist and "pretended" pastors, including self-ordained or self-anointed black preachers and teachers, be authorized, qualified, highly recommended, and licensed by the Governor of the Bahama Islands or a district official. In addition, the particular district and place, chapel or chapels, meeting house or meeting houses considered appropriate (by the colonial authorities) for divine worship, public praying or teaching had to be specified. The license to be a pastor had to be renewed each year.[185] This law was used to create a serious problem for the Reverend Williams.

Three years after becoming the pastor of Bethel Baptist Church, in 1825, supported by a majority of the membership, Williams challenged the sole and arbitrary control of all church money by the trustees whose names were on the original deed to the church's property. The challenge was an effort to em-power the majority of the members and the pastor or a few trustees. One of the trustees, Archibald Parker, who had been a strong advocate in getting the membership to support Pastor Williams' housekeeper living-in arrangements, went to Governor Vesey Munnings, accusing the Reverend Williams of adultery. The Governor's action, sustaining the charge, was swift and final. Prince Williams' license to preach was revoked and his keys to the church taken from him and given to Trustee Parker and Trustee Thomas Reed. Williams, and all the members supporting his position, were "locked out of their church . . . in December 1825."[186] The newspaper columnist, P. Anthony White, previously referred to, made a "tongue-in-check observation" that the "locking out" process "began what may be called the Baptist diaspora in The Bahamas."[187] The Parker-Reed faction replaced the former pastor with Sharper Morris, Prince Williams' friend who had accompanied him in the little open boat from St. Augustine in 1778. Morris became the new pastor of the remaining membership holding possession of the church edifice.

The Reverend Sharper Morris is probably best remembered for his early leadership role in establishing the Baptist witness on Turks Island. About 1830 he sailed to Turks and baptized and organized a group of about fifty people into a church. The people, ridiculed and persecuted by their white masters and neighbors, had been holding religious meetings in uninhabited regions and caves. Morris helped them secure money to purchase land on which they carried an old house to use as a Baptist chapel.[188]

Meanwhile, the intrepid Reverend Williams and the people supporting him were determined to move on. They met for worship and organized a church fellowship in a house on Hospital Lane near the spot where he had begun his outdoor preaching services about forty-five years earlier. They called the new fellowship, St. John's Chapel. A growing membership forced the congregation to move to larger quarters several times. Finally, they settled on a property on which a house was situated, surrounded by a graveyard, located about three hundred yards from the location of Bethel Baptist Church on Meeting Street. They were able to purchase the land in 1832 after receiving a substantial settlement from the Bethel Church trustees and membership. The name on the deed for the land was St. John's Native Baptist Society.

The word "Native" in the church name is a euphemism for "Bahamian." Unlike the Native Baptist Church movement in Jamaica, the name as used by Baptist churches in the Bahamas had little to do with an infusion of Neo-African religious practices and beliefs. In fact, the churches in the Bahamas were never strongly challenged or intimidated by such movements as Myalism in Jamaica, Vodun in Haiti, or Santeria in Cuba.

Three years later, March 1835, the congregation, led by the Reverend Williams, dedicated a stone church edifice with a thatch roof. The present church house, constructed many years later, is situated on the original spot.[189]

St. John Native Baptist Cathedral, Nassau.

An uninvited religious dynamic was introduced into what had been a church movement founded by a former slaves from colonial North America and enthusiastically supported by Afro-Bahamians. Without a request or invitation from the Afro-Bahamian pastors or the members of any church, in 1833, missionaries of the British Missionary Society arrived.

Notes

[177] Symonette and Canzoneri, p. 3.
[178] Ibid., p. 3.
[179] Ibid., pp. 3-4; *Bethel Baptist Bicentennial 1790-1990*, August 5, 1990, p. 11.
[180] C. Powell, Editor, *Bethel Willing Workers Newsletter*, (Nassau: Bethel Baptist Church, Vol. 3, 2002).
[181] Walter H. Brooks, pp. 40-41.
[182] Symonette and Canzoneri, p. 29.
[183] Powell, Bethel Willing Workers Newsletter.
[184] An interview with the Reverend Michaael Symonette in Nassau on January 7, 2000.
[185] Ibid.
[186] Symonette and Canzoneri, p. 18.
[187] White, op cit.
[188] Ibid., p. 11.
[189] Ibid., p. 18.

Chapter Sixteen

THE BRITISH MISSIONARY PRESENCE IN THE BAHAMAS

Uninvited Assistance Graciously Received

The British Missionary Society responded to the letter received from two black Baptist church founders in Jamaica requesting financial aid and missionaries to help them expand Christian evangelism and church development in Western Jamaica and elsewhere by sending the young Reverend John Rowe to Montego Bay in 1814. Rowe's assignment had been to assist two venerable but aging pioneers named George Liele and Moses Baker. That initial decision led the Society to consider, for the first time, an evangelization mission effort throughout the West Indies. Of course, the first and primary BMS mission effort was in Jamaica. The mission work in the Bahama Islands became a most important secondary effort.

Unlike the request and invitation by Liele and Baker, the decision to send missionaries to the Bahamas was a unilateral one. And so, the missionaries arrived in the Bahama Islands, not primarily as evangelists of the "heathen," but as pastors and teachers of existing Baptist Christian communities. Brian Stanley wrote that contact between the black Baptists in the Bahama Islands and the British missionaries was established in 1815 but he failed to stipulate how it was initiated.[190] Sherlock and Bennett, on the other hand, affirm that the decision to include the Bahamas in its foreign work was a unilateral decision of the British Missionary Society at some point, probably after receiving knowledge that there were indigenous Baptist groups already in existence. Had it not been for their knowledge of the substantive organized Baptist church activity among former slaves from North America and Afro-Bahamians (free and slaves) for some time in Nassau and elsewhere, the BMS may have continued to ignore the Bahama Islands. From its inception in 1792, the British Missionary Society, like other foreign mission agencies founded in England (the London Missionary Society founded in 1795 and the British Foreign Bible Society founded in 1803) focused on spreading Christianity in West and South Africa, India, Asia and Australia. The mission efforts in the Caribbean never received its priority attention.[191]

Symonette and Canzoneri contend that when the British missionaries arrived in the Bahamas, in 1833, there were twenty Baptist churches (or societies) already in existence. Joseph Burton and Kilner Pearsons were welcomed by the Bahamian authorities, Anglican and Methodist clergy and the Native Baptist church leaders as well, a political climate quite different from that in Jamaica. Burton had served as the missionary pastor of the East Queen Street Baptist Church in Kingston, Jamaica, and was returning to England because of his wife's deteriorating health. The BMS had requested that he visit Nassau on his way home.

The missionaries invited Sharper Morris (Prince Williams' successor as pastor of Bethel Baptist Church) and Prince Williams (the organizer and pastor of the new St. John's Native Baptist Church) to meet with them. For the first time, Sharper and Williams learned that the Christian church group known as Baptists had originated in England. They also heard that there were very specific theological doctrines and an acceptable process for biblical exegesis.

The British missionaries convinced the two Afro-Bahamian pastors to initiate a policy of modifying their procedures relative to membership requirements (believers baptism, a letter from another orthodox Baptist church), structured (organized worship) and the English Baptist way of church organization. In addition, the missionaries emphasized the requirement that members lead moral lives including being married to and living with one partner. Perhaps the most surprising suggestion accepted by Prince Williams and Sharper Morris related to the format for scheduling

Sunday worship services at which only the British missionaries would preach. Worship was scheduled for Bethel Church each Sunday morning and at St. John's each Sunday afternoon. Church school for all was also to be taught by the missionaries on Sunday evenings in the public school room.[192]

Williams and Morris were so eager to authenticate their churches as orthodox Baptist that they approved the guidelines presented by the British missionaries to completely reorganize them. Prince Williams even agreed to change the name of his church from St. John's Native Baptist Church to St. John's Particular Baptist Church.

Missionary Inspired Crisis and Division

An impasse developed with Prince Williams and the St. John's Church when the Afro-Bahamian pastors and members were urged to sign an "Indorsation" (a statement added to each church's deed that would have made a committee of the British Missionary Society in London associate trustees of both churches). This was an intrusive act that the BMS never attempted in Jamaica. To their credit, Prince Williams, the St. John's membership and other Afro-Bahamian pastors and churches, refused to sign. Obviously, they believed that there was a possibility of the BMS becoming co-owners of the church property with unilateral authority to schedule services and meetings with full responsibility for all teaching, preaching, training and assignments. They suspected that they might end up without any involvement in the decision process for their church.

When analyzed objectively, the attempt by the British missionaries to get Native Baptist pastors and congregations to sign their Indorsement reveals that even as they taught and stressed the necessity of obeying the principles of Baptist church administration and polity to Prince Williams and other Afro-Bahamian pastors, they (Missionaries Burton and Pearsons) were not above modifying those Baptist principles and church polity when it was convenient. They failed to honor one of the cardinal standards of

Baptist Church history which is the principle of local church autonomy, the right of every Baptist church (or congregation) to be independent of outside influence of a person, association, denomination, or another Baptist church. The power, the decision making, rests solely with each Baptist congregation. In the light of history, the former slave who became a pioneer Baptist church evangelist and church founder, Prince Williams, who refused to add the name of the British Missionary Society to the St. John's Church deed, was more "Baptistic" than the theologically-educated, cultured English clergy. Whatever Williams' reasons were for refusing to sign, whether personal or based on his sense of independence and pride, he obviously recognized the attempt to dominate so-called uneducated black leaders and people.

The response of Sharper Morris, Williams' successor at Bethel Baptist Church, was altogether different. Pastor Morris and the Bethel trustees and congregation decided to sign the Indorsation presented by the English missionaries. On December 13, 1834, a committee of the British Missionary Society became associate trustees for the Society of Anabaptists of New Providence (known as Bethel Baptist Church). The names of the Reverends Joseph Burton and Kilner Pearson were placed on the deed to the church property and they became trustees of Bethel Baptist Church. Other Native Baptist pastors and congregations also signed the Indorsation. For five years thereafter, Bethel Church was officially and legally under the direction, or more explicitly, control, domination or regulation of the British Missionary Society. In 1839, one year after the Reverend Burton returned to England, the BMS initiated a deed conveying the title back to the Bethel Board of Trustees alone. However, British missionary influence in some form continued in that church, and in the other churches whose pastor and officers signed the Indorsation, for approximately 100 years.[193]

Another result of the initiative by the British Missionaries to control the Afro-Jamaican Baptist Church movement in the Bahamas was that a pattern was created of two groups of churches: (1) those which were mission congregations—supplied, supported and led by the British Missionary Society personnel, and

(2) those which were independent Afro-Bahamian led Native Baptist Churches. Both types of churches existed in proximity to each other. British Missionary influence in the Bahamas continued until 1931.

A postscript to the Bahamian ministry of the Reverend Joseph Burton is appropriate. Even as he served as the missionary pastor of the Bethel Baptist Church, Burton was involved in building Zion Baptist Church "for whites only" on East Shirley Street in the heart of their settlement in Nassau. When he reported to the Bahamas Baptist Union years later, the Reverend Daniel Wilshere, speaking about Burton, declared, "He turned his back on Bethel and built Zion Church....He never got a white congregation, and it nearly broke his heart; and after seven years he went back to England, a sad and broken man."[194] For several years, Zion Baptist and Bethel Baptist were considered one congregation; Bethel was called Old Chapel and Zion was known as New Chapel.

Although British missionaries after Burton continued to be the official pastors of Bethel, native preachers filled the pulpit on Sunday mornings.[195] Zion Baptist Church became a congregation of Afro-Bahamians who preferred the pastoral leadership of English missionaries. All of Zions pastors, since 1939, have been graduates of the predominantly black American Baptist Theological Seminary and College in Nashville, Tennessee in the United States.

The Concluding Years of Prince Williams

The Reverend Prince Williams, pastor of the independent and autonomous St. John's Particular Church of Native Baptists Society (also the church's present name), was also eager to spread the Christian Gospel beyond the capital city of Nassau and New Providence Island. Supported by his congregation, he traveled to other islands of the Bahamas, encouraging other men to preach the Gospel while organizing Baptist missions, chapels and churches. He was often sharply criticized and persecuted by the

British colonial authorities and Anglican church leaders for preaching, according to them, that John the Baptist was "equal to, if not greater than Jesus Christ." Nevertheless, he, and others from his church, continued preaching and establishing churches until failing health curtailed his efforts. The pioneer black Baptist from North America died in 1840. He was originally buried next to the first Meeting Street church structure on the street named after the church, Meeting Street. In 1914, his grave was relocated and now his remains lie under the baptismal pool of the rebuilt and expanded St. John's Particular Church of Native Baptist Society.[196]

NOTES

[190] Stanley, p. 92.
[191] Sherlock and Bennett, p. 178.
[192] Symonette and Canzoneri, p. 12.
[193] Ibid., pp. 13, 44.
[194] Russell-Bradford, p. 40.
[195] Bicentennial Program, p. 11.
[196] Symonette and Canzoneri, p. 20

Chapter Seventeen

DANIEL WILSHERE: VENERATED BRITISH MISSIONARY – BAHAMIAN CHURCHMAN

A Legendary Ministry Begins

The Baptists of the Bahama Islands regard the legendary Reverend Daniel Wilshere as the most outstanding and honored missionary churchman sent by the British Missionary Society. For fifty-four years, his leadership was critical in creating and promoting the independent Bahamian Baptist Churches throughout the Bahama Islands and the United States. Wilshere resigned a pastorate in Norfolk, England and, accompanied by his wife and two sons, "arrived in Nassau in May 1878 to oversee the native pastors and to develop self-support in the churches." As Superintendent of the district system imposed by earlier missionaries, he found that he was responsible "for the care and development of sixty-eight churches affiliated with the British Missionary Society on twelve Bahama Islands, including New Providence. . . ." Getting to those twelve islands required him to travel "600 miles of voyages, from northwest to southeast, and some 300 miles east and west, most of the Bahama Islands being water. . . ."[197]

Even though he made the prestigious Zion Baptist Church in Nassau his headquarters from the outset, he gave no evidence that he considered his role to be that of a superior white Englishman dealing with inferior black people. Instead, it became obvious to all that Wilshere unreservedly appreciated and respected the Native Baptist ministers, teachers, church leaders and the Afro-Bahamian people in general. He and his wife identified with their struggles and aspirations for Christian knowledge, and their desire to achieve spirituality based on biblical truths while developing dedicated, trained pastoral leadership with self-supporting congregations.

Wilshere and his wife, in turn, were embraced by Native Bahamian Baptists as well as Bahamians who were members of other denominations. He also earned the respect of the English authorities and white community as well. By 1889, the number of churches affiliated with the British Missionary Society increased to eighty-one with 4,352 members.[198] But his pro-active identification with the Bahamians and his unequivocal support of their aspirations led him to question several aspects of British Missionary Society policy. When he traveled to London to report to the home office, he confronted the Society leadership. Reflecting the position of the Bahamian churches leaders, he questioned the Calabar Plan to provide all related churches in the Bahamas with native pastors who were graduates of that school. Calabar College in Kingston, Jamaica, had been founded and was supported by the British Missionary Society to supply Afro-Jamaican church leadership for Jamaica. Of course, Wilshere was himself repudiated by the Society's Board of Directors as a weak administrator for encouraging the Native Baptists to reject plans approved by BMS, the group that was financing them. One year later, Wilshere submitted his letter of resignation to the BMS in London.

The Bahamas Baptist Union

In 1892, when the overwhelming Afro-Bahamian majority of the Zion Baptist Church membership in Nassau rejected Wilshere's missionary replacement for pastoral leadership, Wilshere was official dismissed from the Society. The response of the Bahamian pastors and church leaders was immediate and decisive. On the fifth of April 1892, an all Bahamian committee was convened representing the pastors and majority Afro-Bahamian members of Zion Baptist Church and seventeen representatives from other churches in New Providence and seven other islands. The committee resolved to form the Bahamas Baptist Union (BBU) and invited the Reverend Wilshere to become the first General Superintendent of self-supporting churches. The committee also resolved to send a letter to the Baptist Missionary Society recognizing with appreciation, the many years of commitment and service of its missionaries to the Bahamian people, and Afro-Jamaican Baptist churches in particular. The letter also expressed the hope that financial and missionary support for several churches would continue.

The Society responded by refusing assistance of any kind, leaving the Bahamas Baptist Union to recognize that since July 1891, the Baptist Churches in that island nation were on their own. The Union declared its independence and took steps to carry on the Baptist mission.[199]

Daniel Wilshere's first assignment for the Union was to visit as many Baptist Churches in the United States and Canada as possible to plead for financial assistance. Later, aided by the Mount Carey Baptist Union Church and other Baptist churches in the Bahamas, he launched the construction of the Salem Baptist Union Church on Parliament Street on a lot that had been used as a cow pen. The new church, dedicated in 1894, also served as Bahamas Baptist Union headquarters and his administrative office.

For more than forty years, as the General Superintendent of the Bahamas Baptist Union, Wilshere was an inspiring quintessential leader. One year after the formation of the Union, the number of affiliate churches had grown from fifteen to eighty.[200] Wilshere and his wife sailed to every island in the Bahamas where there was a group of people who desired to organize a Baptist church or wanted to be affiliated with the BBU. Mrs. Wilshere organized schools at Cat island, Exuma and Fox Hill.

Currently, there are about thirty-five churches associated with the BBU. They are located on the Bahama Islands of New Providence, Exuma, Eleuthera and Grand Bahama. Today, reports White, "there are at least nine different Baptist groupings in The Bahamas....Each group is autonomous, with an aggregate of nearly 300 churches scattered through the island . . . the Baptists came together (in 1935) under the umbrella of the Bahamas National Baptist Missionary And Educational Convention. . . ."[201] Over the years the Convention has opened schools, starting with the Jordan School which opened at the Goodwill Centre in Chippingham in 1943 and today is responsible for the Bahamas Baptist Community College, the CW Saunders School, the Jordan Prince Williams High School, and the Bahamas Baptist Institute and Seminary.

Bahama Baptist Union Mission Churches in the United States

The first Baptist church for Bahamians living in the United States was organized by the Bahamas Baptist Union one hundred and thirty-four years after the pioneer Baptist preacher named Prince Williams arrived in Nassau harbor. In 1912, Superintendent Daniel Wilshere received urgent requests from Bahamians who had immigrated to the United States by the hundreds. From the 1870s to the first decade of the twentieth century they had lived in Key West, Florida. When the cigar industry declined after 1910, they moved north to Miami for employment in the hotel and railway system of Henry Flagler. Until 1917 there were few immigration restrictions to bar entry of male migrant workers and labors. Initially it had been the young able-bodied men who migrated directly to Miami, leaving their families in the Bahama Islands.[202] They longed for a Bahamian church environment in which they would feel at home. Wilshere and the Bahamas Baptist Union responded by establishing the Mt. Olive Baptist *Union* Church in Miami. By 1924 there were six (additional) BBU related churches in Florida: five in Miami and one in West Palm Beach. All were led by ministers who were of Bahamian heritage and educated in the Bahamas and the United States.[203] The word *Union* in the name of their churches denotes their Bahamian membership and their affiliation with the Bahamas Baptist Union. Other Union churches, all in Florida, are: St. Matthew Missionary Baptist *Union* Church and the Temple Missionary Baptist *Union* Church in Miami, and New Hope Missionary Baptist *Union* Church in Goulds.

The Baptist religious cultural gospel thread has come full circle. Many of the immigrant Bahamians were responding to spiritual needs that were theirs because of the life of Prince Williams, a former slave preacher who was consumed by a zeal to share Christianity with people of African descent in the Bahama Islands.

Notes

[197] Russell-Bradford, pp. 39, 51.
[198] Symonette and Canzoneri, pp. 38, 39.
[199] Russell-Backford, pp. 10, 11. (The information summarized above was taken from the Declaration of Independence drawn up the Bahamas Baptist Union.)
[200] Ibid., p. 14.
[201] Ibid.
[202] Howard Johnson, *The Bahamas in Slavery and Freedom* (Kingston: Ian Publishers Limited, 1991), p. 169.
[203] Symonette and Conzoneri, p. 49.

Chapter Eighteen

THE LEGACY OF PRINCE WILLIAMS AND OTHER BAPTISTS

A Contemporary Evaluation of Prince Williams and the Baptists

Accompanied by Sharper Morris, Williams sailed from St. Augustine (East Florida), benching their little sail boat on the beach in Nassau Harbor. He planted the seeds that became Bethel Baptist Church and St. John's Particular Native Baptist Church, two of the founding churches of the Bahamas Baptist Union and all other Native Baptist churches. A Bahamian newspaper columnist by the name of P. Anthony White, has written that the lifestyles of Prince Williams and Daniel Wilshire "and so much in those early years of budding Christianity...(in the Bahamas)...were forecasts of a modern day when Baptists would look back and appreciate that their history is indeed richer in the milk of humanity than the honey of rituals."[204] Some achievements and legacies of the Bahamian Baptists of which all Bahamians should be proud, combined with elements of English law, form the bedrock of Bahamian society and culture. They are the "milk of humanity" the columnist referred to.

(1) When people from other countries and continents comment with surprise about how peacefully and regularly elections are held throughout the Bahama Islands, they unknowingly praise the Baptists of the yesteryears. Those Baptist ministers, Afro-Jamaican and British missionary, not only fought to guarantee the right of self-government but also started free schools for all their free and slave members who were taught reading, writing and Christian principles on Sunday evenings. For the most part,

they were poor and landless. Although Sandra Riley provides evidence that a free black Methodist minister, Joseph Paul, was the first master (principal) of the private Associates School for blacks in Nassau, it was open only to a limited few.[205] Methodist missionaries also opened schools for their church members.

(2) Baptist ministers, in cooperation with Methodist and Presbyterian clergy, fought for and secured the freedom for all religions, denominations and sects to freely preach the gospel and worship without having to obtain the permission of the government, civil authorities or a state (Anglican) church.[206]

(3) A Baptist minister, the Reverend Henry Capern, in 1841, led the struggle to eliminate the indentured process, whereby persons had to pay for being transported to the Bahama Islands by obligating themselves to work for a designated number of years. The same law gave indentured persons the freedom to join the church or religious group of their choice.[207]

(4) Because of the tireless efforts of the Baptists, a law was passed in 1824 encouraging marriages between slaves and between slaves and free persons. This law evolved into the recognition of marriage for all people notwithstanding race, religion or pre-existing condition.[208]

(5) British missionaries and Afro-Bahamian ministers joined other clergy to establish the right for all ministers, white and black, to perform marriages if they were associated and recognized by a known religious group. All clergy were also permitted to conduct funerals and bury persons of all colors and religious persuasions in graves on public land. Those privileges had previously been reserved for Anglican clergy.[209]

All of the freedoms and privileges mentioned, initially fought for by Afro-Jamaican ministers and British missionaries, have been incorporated, indeed, form the basis of the Constitution of the Bahama Islands. Afro-Bahamians and people from the nearby island of Haiti and other continents who enjoy the economic and retirement opportunities available in the Bahama Islands, have delighted in the garden of liberation, and equal access and treatment under law and may even consider them islands of paradise.

Pioneer Preachers in Paradise
Bahamian Baptist: A Summary

Two African-American Baptist missionary preachers, the Reverend Gorge Liele and Moses Baker, after thirty-one years of successful Christian evangelism and church organization, invited the British Missionary Society to send financial aid and missionaries to Jamaica to help them. As a result of that initial interest in Jamaica the British began to contemplate additional islands for Baptist missions. They heard that several untrained and non-ordained former slave preachers, the Reverend Prince Williams and others from the British colonies in North America, had succeeded in planting seeds of Baptist Christianity in the Bahama Islands. A missionary returning to England after an abbreviated mission tour in Jamaica was asked to investigate. Neither the missionary nor any representative of the British Missionary Society had been invited by the pastors or lay leaders of the Bahamian Baptist churches. Upon arrival, the British missionaries found thriving, organized congregations and many church edifices. For the most part, the black pioneers and Afro-Bahamian churches welcomed them and their knowledge of the Bible and Baptist polity and the British missionaries helped establish policies and build a foundation that has withstood the test of the years.

The Baptist legacy (Afro-Bahamian and British missionary) is reflected in the statistics of the 2002 Bahamian Census reports. Baptists compose the largest religious denomination. Baptists constitute 32 percent of the population of approximately 298,000 people.[210]

Since Bahamian Independence (1973) Baptists have held prominent leadership positions in the national government. Twenty-nine years after Independence (2003), according to the Reverend John Roker, a retired Baptist minister now living in Florida and one of the leading activists in the early struggle for Bahamian independence, all of the following who hold high political office in the Bahamian government are Baptists: the Honorable Houbert Christie, Prime Minister; Cynthia Pratt, Deputy Prime Minister; Ivy Dumont, Governor General; and Alma

Adams, Counsel General (Miami). Madam Alma Adams' father was a leading Baptist minister and denominational historian. This record of these and other Baptist leaders and churches who in many ways are living testaments of their pioneer Baptist heritage should be known and affirmed by Baptists the world over.

NOTES

[204] A quote during a personal interview of the Reverend Michael C. Symonette, from an article written by P. Anthony White in a local newspaper, (Nassau, January 7, 2000)

[205] Sandra Riley, p. 11.

[206] Symonette and Conzoneri, p. 32.

[207] Ibid., p. 49.

[208] Ibid., p. 29.

[209] Ibid., p. 45.

[210] *World Almanac 2002*, p. 772.

PART III
Baptist Origins and Development in Haiti

Chapter Nineteen

THOMAS PAUL: AFRICAN-AMERICAN BAPTIST MISSIONARY

Paul's Early Years in Boston

The invisible but undeniably religious-cultural gospel thread of Christianity that connects the descendants of African people living in the United States with descendants of Africans living in Haiti was first extended by Thomas Paul. Born in Exeter, New Hampshire on September 3, 1773, Paul's parents were blacks who may have occasionally been taken to be Caucasoid. They attended a Baptist church with a predominately white congregation. The celebrated historian, Carter G. Woodson, identified Paul as a white person, and wrote that at age sixteen, in 1789, he was baptized by the pastor of the church, a Reverend Mr. Lock.[211]

Later that year, in Boston, Massachusetts, Paul joined a group of blacks who, for over a decade, had been meeting for worship and informal discussions in private homes. That was their way of protesting segregating seating in "Negro Pews" and the hypocritical religious racism they endured when they attended the predominately white First and Second Baptist Churches. Since the early years of slavery, slaves and free blacks had been granted a limited membership status that permitted them to be baptized and attend worship services but prohibited them from speaking, singing or participating in church activities. Because their "protest" group had grown in number, they had been granted the use of a building called Faneuil Hall for religious purposes on Tuesday and Friday afternoons.

Paul, who may have been considering becoming a minister before attending Harvard College, impressed the members of the

First African Baptist Church, Boston (a.k.a. Joy Street Meeting House).

worship and discussion groups with his knowledge of the Bible. Even at his young age, he had the ability to interpret clearly and discuss passages in the New and Old Testaments. The members encouraged him to assume the role of "exhorter" or biblical advisor

The First African (a.k.a. Joy Street) Baptist Church

The year 1805 was an eventful one for Thomas Paul, by then thirty-two years of age. He became a recognized preacher for an increasing group of black, and several white, worshipers. On May 1, 1805, Paul was ordained as a Baptist minister by the Reverend Locke in West Nottingham, New Hampshire. Three months later, on August 8, with officers and members of both First and Second Baptist Churches of Boston present, Paul and the membership of twenty were officially constituted as the First African Baptist Church. It was also the first independent Baptist church for people of color in the northern section in the United States.

On December 4, 1805, a church edifice (known as the African Meeting house) was constructed by all-Black laborers on Belknap, later and presently known as Joy Street. Even though the church is identified by some historians as Joy Street Baptist Church, the names First African Baptist Church and African Meeting House are used by the Boston Museum of Afro-American History. Whatever its name, the Reverend Thomas Paul was installed as its first pastor on December 4, 1806.[212] In addition to the development of its religious services and educational activities the new church became a place for celebrations and political and anti-slavery meetings. White citizens of Boston also attended the various services held at the church, attracted by Paul's preaching. They participated freely in all church activities.[213] By 1819 the membership had increased to 103.

Paul's influence and the aid and assistance of the membership extended to black church groups in other cities and states. The church officially gave its pastor permission to travel extensively. Everywhere the gifted young minister appeared, he attracted large crowds. Under the impact of his "pleasing and fervid addresses" and preaching, many people were converted and baptized. Others joined the crowds because "his color excited considerable curiosity.[214] Paul's participation in the meetings and services of the Boston Baptist Association resulted in invitations to preach and conduct lecture series in predominantly white Baptist churches throughout the northeastern area of the United States and elsewhere. It is believed that in 1815 he was invited to travel to England where he preached to zealous anti-slavery supporters. If so, the well-known and highly acclaimed pioneer Baptist, the Reverend George Liele, may not have been the first black Baptist minister to preach in England. That honor may go to the Reverend Thomas Paul.

Organizing Abyssinian Baptist Church (NYC)

While conducting a lecture series in New York City, Paul became involved with a group of blacks, many of whom originally came from the East African area called Abyssinia, now Ethiopia. They had been worshiping for some time at the predominately white First Baptist Church. Seating for blacks, as in Boston and most white churches everywhere, was limited to the balcony or designated segregated areas. The group pleaded with the Reverend Paul to help them organize an independent congregation. The members of First African (or Joy Street) Baptist Church in Boston granted their pastor a three-month leave of absence to organize the discontented blacks into the Abyssinia Baptist Fellowship in 1808. When the pastor and members of First Baptist Church were satisfied that Paul's teaching and church organization were orderly (grounded in Biblical doctrine and Baptist principles) they granted honorable letters of dismissal to four men and twelve women. They, along with three others, were constituted a gospel church on Wednesday, July 5, 1809 known as the Abyssinian Baptist Church, the first independent African-American congregation in New York City.

PIONEER PREACHERS IN PARADISE

Paul's Interest in the People of Haiti

One of the factors that caused Thomas Paul to become interested in the people of Haiti was the news of the slave rebellion, abolition of slavery and the establishment of an independent black nation a few hundred miles south of the United States. In 1791 when the black masses first rose up against the Spanish, the English and finally the French, Paul was eighteen years old. He was greatly influenced by the reports that circulated throughout New England. News of the revolution greatly impacted the social and economic conditions of blacks, especially in New York City where slavery was not legally abolished until July 4, 1827. A. Roi Ottley and William J. Weatherby help us to understand some of the significant factors that impacted black people.

First, the revolt of the slaves in Haiti awakened Northern blacks anew "to the great dream of liberty. . . . Long yearning for a Moses, Negroes found him at last in the distant but heroic figure of Toussaint l'Ouverture. . . ." Second, the Haitian slave uprising catapulted the "Negro Problem" into the public scene as a national issue with pro-slavery supporters proclaiming that increasing slave insurrections in the United States were being inspired and attributed to Haitian blacks who, in Haiti, were accused of inflicting horrendous savage acts against their white slave masters. Third, as slavery as an institution was declining in the north eastern parts of the United States, anti-Negro campaigns resorted to intense acts of prejudice and racism. No person with the "slightest tincture of Negro blood, or tinge of complexion" was permitted to mingle with whites. "This form of prejudice was early symbolized in New York (and Boston) by installing "Negro Pews" in the churches."[215]

Ottley and Weatherby also point out that "not the least of the effects produced by the Haitian upheaval was the emotion which it aroused...the wondrous tales of bravery . . . the courage of the black men of Haiti." A significant factor in the development of a new "race consciousness among American blacks, north and south, was the discovery of "a new kinship with blacks all over the world." What the blacks of Haiti succeeded in accomplishing "created a national Negro movement in the United States. . . ."[216]

African-American Migration to Haiti

It is extremely likely that Thomas Paul became knowledgeable and deeply interested in the invitation of the new Haitian leaders like the popular and flamboyant Henri Christophe and President Jean-Boyer who urged skilled free blacks and slaves to migrate to their country. Christophe is seldom mentioned in American history books nor is he appreciated by many for bringing a large contingent of well trained and disciplined veteran Haitian soldiers to the United States to stand with General Andrew Jackson in the defense of New Orleans against the British military in 1814. Paul probably was aware that blacks who accepted the offer of the Haitian leaders were offered full citizenship and, as an additional incentive, thousands of acres of land that had already been set aside for them to occupy without cost. Bishop Richard Allen of the African Methodist Episcopal Church strongly endorsed migration and upwards to 13,000 blacks, many of them members of the AME Church did so in 1823, responding to the appeal of President Jean-Pierre Boyer.

Finally, Paul may have been concerned, that because Baptists in England and the United States were already strongly committed to support evangelistic and missionary efforts in West Africa, the spiritual needs of the blacks for Baptist church development in Haiti might be overlooked.

Paul's Mission Evaluation Plan for Haiti

In spite of his understanding that Baptists of North America (United States and Canada) had not developed plans to establish mission efforts in Haiti, on March 5, 1823, he wrote a letter to the Massachusetts Baptist Missionary Society expressing his concern about the spiritual plight of that island. In fact, the MBMS had been founded in 1802 by representatives of Baptist Churches in Boston to furnish occasional preaching and the promotion of knowledge of evangelistic truth in the new settlements within the United States. However, the scope of its responsibilities could be expanded to include other areas of the world if the mission society considered it proper. Item 21 of the handwritten minutes of the Society notes, "Read a letter from Rev. Tho. Paul requesting a mission to Haiti." Item 22 reads, "Voted to give him a mission for six months, and that his mission expenses be 200 dollars."[217]

Obviously Paul believed that a six-month period would give him the opportunity to investigate adequately, evaluate, and determine the feasibility and priority of establishing a permanent Baptist mission in the twenty-year-old independent but impoverished black governed nation. He was too optimistic. The reality was that he would encounter tremendous handicaps. The overwhelming majority of the Haitian blacks, less than two decades removed from brutal slave conditions, were illiterate. Except for Cap Haitian and Port-au-Prince, it was an undeveloped country that was rural and mountainous. Paul was a light-skinned African American born, raised and sheltered in predominately white New England who had attended Harvard College but was unable to communicate with the Haitian masses whose language was Creole. With those handicaps, one wonders whether the reason the Massachusetts Baptist Missionary Society approved such a venture was due to the limited expenditure it required and the popularity of Thomas Paul himself in the Boston area.

The Society and others helped Paul secure a large number of Bibles and religious tracts written in French and Spanish. The American Bible Society prepared a special copy of the Bible to present to the President of Haiti. On March 31, 1823, Thomas Paul embarked from Boston Harbor. He was the first African-American Baptist missionary destined to the island of Haiti.[218]

NOTES

[211] Carter G. Woodson, *The History of the Negro Church* (Washington, D. C.: The Associated Publishers, 3rd ed., 1972), p. 76.

[212] John Oliver and Lois E. Horton, *Black Bostonians* (New York: Holmes and Meier Publishers, Inc., Revised Edition, 1979), P. 42.

[213] *Boston African-American National Historic Site,* Boston African-

American National Historic Site, *The Black Heritage Trail* (Boston: Museum of Afro-American History, Fall, 2000 and Winter 2000-2001), p. 4.

[214] Woodson, p. 76.

[215] A. Roi Ottley and William J. Weatherby, *The Negro In New York* (Dobbs Ferry New York: Oceana Publications, Inc., 1967), pp. 45-50.

[216] Ibid., pp. 51-52.

[217] The Minutes of the Massachusetts Baptist Missionary Society (Cambridge: March 5, 1823) p. 215.

[218] Charles Poisset Romain, *Le Protestantisme Dans La Society Haitienne* (Paris: Imprimene: Henri Deschamps, 1986), p. 57; Docteur C. Pressoir, *Le Protestantisme Haitien, 2e Vol.* (Haiti: Imprimerie du Seminaire Adventiste, 1976), p. 109.

Chapter Twenty

HAITI BEFORE THOMAS PAUL: 1492 TO 1832

European Colonization

When Christopher Columbus was directed to an island the natives called Hayti (which meant "mountain land"), he was looking for gold not sugar or rum or vacation retreats featuring white beaches and warm sunshine filled days. Columbus called the island, Hispaniola. The "uncivilized" native Arawak people warmly welcomed him, his soldiers and the Roman Catholic priests who were in his party. The Tainos, as they were called, initially thought the Spaniards were from heaven. They were "rewarded" for their hospitality by being forced to labor for their uninvited "civilized" usurpers without compensation. They were introduced to Christianity, strange and, for them, deadly European diseases and artificial famine caused by the destruction of their crops when they rose up in rebellion. In time, the superior armed Spaniards reduced the Arawak Indians from an estimated more than fifty thousand population to about six thousand in a period of fifteen years.[219]

Other estimates about the destruction of the native population suggest that between three hundred thousand and one million died of exhaustion, disease, violence or suicide between 1492 and 1550. The exhaustion of the river beds and mines further led the Spaniards to move West toward newer eldorados in what are today Mexico and Peru.[220]

The desolation of the native population that had, when the Spaniards arrived, been friendly and helpful, intensely moved Las Calas, a Roman Catholic Dominican priest. When he returned to

Spain he pleaded with Spanish government officials to import Africans to end the destruction of the island natives. The Africans, Las Calas argued, would end the destruction of the natives while providing the slave labor needed to mine the gold the Spaniards thought would make Spain a rich and powerful nation. The Spanish government listened to the pleas of the highly respected Dominican spiritual father for a "holy" alliance between "the State" and "the Christian Church." King Charles V responded and by royal edict, in 1517, the Atlantic Slave Trade began, a very profitable 350-year enterprise that sold millions of Africans into an unholy and inhuman status of perpetual bondage.[221]

In 1695, Spain was forced to divide the island and give the western third to the French who established settlements there. That island area has been known as St. Domingue and San Domingo. The former may be the more accurate name since the eastern two-thirds of the island that remained under Spanish control is now called the Dominican Republic.

African Slave Buildup and Development

By 1697, the combined population of St. Domingue was 56,000 slaves from Africa and 6,000 European adults. Philip Curtin, in his definitive analysis of the North Atlantic Slave Trade, estimates that from 1451 to 1802, more than 864,000 Africans were thrown into the slave labor force in St. Domingue, more than twice the number shipped to what is now the United States.[222] That number included slaves directly from Africa and from British colonies (like Jamaica) in the Caribbean.[223] The plantation system produced a variety of agricultural products, the most important being sugar and sugar products such as molasses and rum.

A major problem developed because the colonial plantation system that relied heavily on slave labor to maintain its economic base in the Caribbean, did not have a slave tradition to support it. Frank Tannenbaum points out that the French did not have a slave tradition to refer to. A legacy of slave law was nonexistent. Unlike the Spanish and Portuguese, the French did not develop a set of religious principles to accommodate the enslavement of Africans. Instead, they embraced a document known as the Code Noir (Black Code) that defined slave policy. The code officially recognized an institution that had been functioning for fifty years without the approval of the French government. All slaves were defined not as persons but as a special kind of property or "things."[224] Joan Dayan of the University of Arizona, calls the code "the most barbaric produce of the Enlightenment."[225] The Black Code was never printed in the English language. The political activist and writer, Eric Williams, wrote that the Code Noir not only gave legal sanction to the institution of slavery but made provisions for the governing of the slaves as follows: "All slaves were to be baptized, only Roman Catholics could have charge of slaves, . . . (and) . . . marriages...were to be encouraged and father and mother being replaced by consent of the owner. . . ."[226]

According to James, the most humane aspect of the Code Noir was, that while it forbade slave assemblies except for Roman Catholic worship, it mandated that two hours in the middle of each day and work free Sundays and feast days belonged to the slaves so that they would have time to cultivate a small parcel of land on which to grow foods to supplement their regular rations. The most diligent and ambitious slaves were thereby able to raise vegetables, chickens and pigs, not only for food, but also for rum, tobacco, or to accumulate enough money to purchase their freedom.[227] However, Williams argues that "The Code forbade the ownership of property by slaves...(who were) forbidden . . . to sell, publically or privately, any other kinds of produce without permission."[228]

In spite of the Codes' few humane aspects, the overwhelming number of French planters and Roman Catholic priests on St. Domingue were indifferent about the slaves' welfare. Principles of religion were sacrificed in the interest of sound economic policies. The Governor of Martinique observed that, for the safety of the whites, slaves had to be "kept in profound ignorance . . . and . . . treated like beasts."[229] Only a few priests identified with the slave community and labored with them in their struggle, and, as we shall see, even fought side by side with them against the French during the years of revolt and revolution. And yet, in spite of the standard for treatment of slaves promoted by the French colonial government, planters and the majority of Roman priests, there were Jesuits, brothers of the Society of Jesus, who encouraged the slaves to rebel until they were expelled from the island. Within a few years, a report to Rome noted that citizens and slaves had lost all the sentiments of religion they had gained from the Jesuits.[230]

Notes

[219] C.L.R. James, *The Black Jacobins* (New York: Random House, 1963), p. 4.

[220] From the Internet: pasture.enc.purdue.edu/-agenhtlml/ agen-mc/Haiti/history.html; 10/27/2000.

[221] Ibid., p. 4.

[222] Curtin, p. 88.

[223] James, p. 53.

[224] Frank Tannenbaum, *The Destiny of the Negro in the Western Hemisphere* (Political Science Quarterly, March 1946).

[225] Joan Dayan, *Haiti; History and the Gods* (Berkeley/Los Angeles: University of California Press, 1998), p. 201.

[226] Eric Williams, *From Columbus to Castro: The History of the Caribbean, 1492-1969* (New York: Harper and Ross, 1970, p. 183.

[227] James, p. 11; Simpson, p. 64.

[228] Williams, p. 184.

[229] Williams, p. 1; James, p.11.

[230] James G. Leburn, *The Haitian People* (New Haven: Yale University Press, 1941), pp. 116-117.

Chapter Twenty-One

THE SLAVE'S RELIGION: A CONTRIBUTING FACTOR FOR REVOLT

The Development of Vodun (or Voodoo)

Another Neo-African religious system developed and persevered in European West Indian slave-based colonies where slaves greatly outnumbered the whites but existed almost totally isolated from them. That separation was especially true in St. Domingue (Haiti). On the other hand, the African presence among the slaves remained dominant because the importation of slave labor was promoted for over a three-hundred-year period. Newly arrivals, mostly adult males from West Africa, especially Dahomey (now Benin) and the Yoruba Empire (now Nigeria), continually strengthened African religious traditions.

Vodun (or Voodoo) is the Fon tribal name of a religious possession group. It is also the general name for all folk religions in Dahomey. Slaves from Dahomey were the most numerous and dominant tribal group, therefore their predominant "deities" along with "deities" from other tribal groups represented in the slave population, were resurrected to become the basis of their religion in their existential environment. Luc de Heusch notes, as required by the Code Noir, as they were exposed to Roman Catholicism worship and practice, "the slaves adapted their (African) customs to (their) new circumstances and environment, using Afro-Creole religion as an integral form of their resistance to European (white) domination."[231] More than a syncretism of Dahomey beliefs and Roman Catholicism, in Vodun ceremonies, the Roman Catholic saint "is not a front, a mask that hides the (African) god . . . since African signs and emblems prevail. Believers in Vodun are baptized and participate without any contradiction in Catholic masses. . . . Two distinct religions coexist without merging. Catholic influences are superficial in Vodun whose reality is African."[232]

Even though nonparticipants of Vodun find it difficult to understand, unquestionably the slaves in Haiti received several important benefits from their religion. First, their Neo-African religion was a faith vehicle that united them spiritually. Second, it provided the integral form of their resistance to French and slave master's domination. Fisk, for example, notes that "Voodoo...provided slaves with amulets (and other things) believed to protect the holder against any harm while committing an act of resistance that was justified by his religion. . . ." Because the practice was forbidden by their slave masters, "Voodoo was practiced clandestinely...it helped to create and sustain an atmosphere of terror that tended at times to lock the planter in a state of psychological insecurity, if not paranoia."[233] The whites intuitively believed, and rightly so, that Vodun was their slaves' medium of conspiracy. When the slaves danced and sang in their secret midnight gatherings, one of the songs they sang for over two hundred years was, when translated from their Creole, "We swear to destroy the whites and all they possess; let us die rather than fail to keep this vow."[234] The slaves sang even though the planters and colonial authorities tried desperately to stamp out their religion, its leaders and its music.

A third benefit of their religion was the formation of a dream of freedom against severe seemingly unsurmountable odds. Fourthly, Vodun, initially provided and often undergirded the leadership that helped liberate them from the physical degradation of their condition.

Slave Leadership from Revolt (1791) to Independence (1802)

The struggle to gain their freedom lasted for thirteen years. The slaves in Haiti fought against trained and superior armed colonial forces and from time to time, groups of free blacks and Mulattos. They also had to contend against professional soldiers from Spain and England, the two nations which wanted to reclaim the prosperous island (from France) during the periods of slave unrest and revolt. Notwithstanding the odds, the slaves resisted, fought and finally defeated the English, Spanish and the French army of Napoleon Bonaparte whose goal was always to maintain black enslavement and protect valuable French sugar interests, a cornerstone of the French economy.

The slave who gave significant leadership to the first organized revolt of any consequence was an illiterate Voodoo priest (Papaloi) named Boukman.[235] In a service near Le Cap or Cap Francais (now Cap Haitian) in northern St. Domingue on the night of August 20, 1791, that included frenzy incantations and sucking the blood of a stuck pig, Boukman incited his followers to pull down the cross, symbol of the white god, and kill every white man, woman and child. In fact, many whites were spared by the revolting slaves, including priests whom they feared and physicians who had been kind to them. Throughout the area hundreds of plantations were burned and totally destroyed. In few days, however, Boukman was captured by the French and hanged, but the revolt continued. About one month after Boukman's death, a tall black "slave" named Toussaint from the plantation of a humane owner named Breda joined the rebellion.

Toussaint L'Ouverture

Toussaiant's father was the son of a low ranking African chief who was captured and sold into slavery in West Africa. Brought to St. Domingue, he was purchased by an owner who recognized that he was unusual and allowed him certain liberties on the plantation. He was exposed to and became a Roman Catholic. Married by a priest, he fathered and raised eight children. Toussaint, the oldest, was taught to respect African traditions and understand the medicinal value of herbs and plants as were all African tribal leaders. An old black, named Pierre Baptiste, greatly influenced Toussaint. Baptiste taught him to read and write, the principles of geometry and even the rudiments of Latin by using the services of the Catholic Church as a guide. That knowledge and Toussaint's basic intelligence led his owner, an unusually humane and generous man, to promote him from herdsman to coachman and finally, to steward of all the livestock on the plantation. Toussaint learned to speak and negotiate with whites on a day to day basis. He learned to be deferential and passive yet crafty and resourceful when dealing with whites and blacks. He found it necessary to study the psychological make-up of the master while not permitting anyone, including fellow slaves, to know his inner thoughts and desires. Throughout his life, he regarded whites and blacks with a certain disdain, never placing full confidence in anyone.[236]

Toussaint's religious experiences as a Roman Catholic always provided the strict parameters for all the decisions he made. Throughout his life, he never attended anything but Catholic worship service - his demeanor that of a devout believer guided by the religious teaching of the Dominican Catechism. The opportunities provided by his owner to become acquainted with whites and at the same time develop leadership skills among whites and blacks in addition to his strict religious beliefs are helpful in attempting to understand the seeming contradictions in Toussaints's behavioral responses to various life situations. He never seemed to "emancipate himself decisively from the white man (nor) fully embrace the cause of blacks" and their commitment to non-Christian, neo-African religious deities.[237]

Toussaint always equated freedom with the privilege of being a free Frenchman. As a devout Roman Catholic, and even as he was involved in the struggle to define himself, his fervent desire was that everyone one, slaves and others, could wear the double crown of freedom and French citizenship. Becoming French, culturally and politically, was the only way a slave and mulatto people could ever rise up to claim the best of civilization. Interestingly, that concept was not an ideal that was religiously inspired but the result of reading a book recommended by his slave tutor, Baptiste.

The book, written by a French priest named Abbe Raynal, became his political guide. In it, Father Raynal boldly called for a slave revolution to relieve Africa and Africans. Toussaint was deeply moved by the idea that natural liberty was a right given to every person. When Raynal declared that slavery was an instrument in the hands of wickedness and that only a courageous chief was needed in Haiti, Toussaint began to visualize that he was that chief.[238]

Father Raynal was probably influenced by a group of intellectuals in France like Jean-Jacques Rousseau and Francois-Marie Voltaire who were considered as Friends of Negroes. The group was setting forth ideas that formed the basis of the revolution against the King of France by the middle-class and eventually the poor masses. The slogan for the revolution was Liberty, Equality, and Fraternity. Those principles were adopted by Toussaint and may have been the rationale for his joining the slave revolt started by Boukman. At that decisive juncture in his life, he began to call himself, Toussaint L'Ouverture. A few months later he was the recognized Commander-in-Chief of the revolutionary slave army. From the very beginning, even though as Commander-in-Chief, L'Ouverture constantly declared that the practice of Voodoo was strictly forbidden, there is no record that his followers obeyed. No one was ever punished for continuing to acknowledge Voodoo deities or attending their secret ceremonies.

When he appointed himself Governor of Haiti, an appointment approved by Napoleon Bonaparte, one of L'Ouverture's first tasks was to write Haiti's first constitution in which slavery was abolished.[239] His constitution also sharply reduced the influence of the Roman Catholic Church by strictly subordinating it to the state (or nation). The Governor was to portion to each priest or religious leader the extent of his administration. All clergy were forbidden to form associations of any kind. The Governor also was given the authority to censor all printed matter.[240]

Haitian Leaders after Toussaint L'Ouverture: A Mixed Bag

After Toussaint was deceived by the French military commander and taken into captivity (along with his family), he was transported to France and imprisoned. As a prisoner, he died in 1804. When he left Haiti, he was succeeded by one of his generals, Jean-Jacques Dessalines, who quickly proclaimed himself Emperor for Life. He was the first of many self-appointed leaders who came to power as military generals and appointed themselves Emperors or Presidents, "for Life." Dessalines was the first to openly practice and promote Vodun. Later, Faustin Soulouque, who ruled Haiti for seventeen years (1847 to 1864), actually brought his personal resident bocor (high priest) and houngan (priest) into the National Palace. For the first time, national leaders placed the mark of acceptability on a Neo-African religion in the Western Hemisphere. Usually, Haiti had two national state religions; one Euro-based Roman Catholicism; the other Afro-centric Vodun.[241] Other national leaders duplicated the policy of their President or Emperor, practicing Vodun openly and honorably or Roman Catholicism as required. One-hundred-twenty-seven years later, President Jean-Bertrand Aristide, a former Roman Catholic priest, not only recognizes Voodoo as a religion but a priestess bestowed a presidential sash on him at his first inauguration in 1991.[242]

To match the cruelty of the French military, Dessalines resorted to the techniques of the anti-Christian Voodoo inspired Boukman. The Emperor encouraged his army to carry out indiscriminate and merciless slaughter of thousands of whites living in the country. Those who were not slaughtered fled to France and the United States, taking with them the management skills, resources, knowledge and production experience so critical if Haiti was to revitalize and reestablish its destroyed sugar, coffee and rice economy. Haiti has been a poverty prone, poor, independent black island nation ever since.

"Emperor for Life" Dessalines was assassinated in 1807 and Haiti was divided between two men who had also been revolutionary generals under L'Ouverture. Henri Christophe ruled in the northern part of the country and Alexander Petion in the west and south. Both were practicing Roman Catholics. Christophe is remembered mainly for building the fortress-palace he called the Citadel on the summit of Mt. Milot located south-west of Cap Haitian. But, secretly, he corresponded with English Anglicans (known as Episcopalians in the United States) and Methodist

Wesleyan church leaders such as William Wilberforce, requesting them to send people to Haiti to preach and teach Protestantism. Christophe's plan was to use the Protestant religious groups to abolish all vestiges of French colonialism and break the control and influence of Roman Catholicism which had never been committed to improving the conditions of his impoverished countrymen.[243]

John-Pierre Boyer, was the President of Haiti when the Reverend Thomas Paul arrived at Cap Haitian in 1823 for his six-month inspection and missionary feasibility study tour. However, the first Protestant Christians to reach Haiti were John Brown and James Catts of the Wesleyan Methodist Church from Bristol, England who arrived six years previously, responding to the call of Henri Christophe.[244] The first black Baptists may have been immigrants from the Bahama Islands. Among that group is believed to have been a man named Tredwell who may have received authorization from the Haitian government to build a chapel. It is not certain that he was an ordained minister.[245] An African Methodist Episcopal Church (AME) under the leadership of Bishop Richard Allen, was formally established in Haiti in 1832 in response to repeated requests from members of that denomination who were among the 13,000 black immigrants from the United States. President Boyer had guaranteed them religious freedom and prime land to occupy.[246]

NOTES

[231] Luc de Heusch, "King Kong in Haiti: A New Approach to Religious Syncretism" in *Slavery and Beyond, The African Impact on Latin America and the Caribbean,* ed. Darien J. Davis, (Wilmington: Scholarly Research, Inc., 1995), p. 103.
[232] Ibid, p. 106.
[233] Fick, p. 66.
[234] James, p. 18.
[235] James, p. 90.
[236] George F. Tyson, Jr., *Toussaint L'Ouverture* (Englewood Cliffs:

Prentice Hall, Inc., 1973), pp. 12, 14 (and James, pp. 119, 120.
[237]Tyson, p. 14.
[238]James, p. 25.
[239]Ibid., pp. 153, 264.
[240]Ibid., 264.
[241]Robert D. Heinl and Nancy G. Heinl, *Written In Blood: The Study of the Haitian People* (Lanham, Maryland: University Press of America, 1996), p. 197.
[242]Michael Morton, "Haiti Gives Voodoo Its Blessing," *The Star Ledger* (Newark, New Jersey: 11 April 2003, p. 8.
[243]Romain, p. 50.
[244]Ibid., p. 51.
[245]Pressoir, p. 109.
[246]Ibid., p. 8.

Chapter Twenty-Two
BAPTIST MISSIONS IN HAITI

Thomas Paul: An Unrelenting Mission Plan

Thomas Paul was the first recognized ordained black Baptist missionary from North America to arrive in Haiti with the endorsement of an official Baptist Missionary Society. His base of operations was Cap Haitian where he was warmly received by Haitian customs officials. He found a young independent black nation beset with serious problems, probably unknown to Paul.

One of the problems was sectionalism—the people of Haiti were more loyal to the north or south and west rather than to the nation itself. Sectional loyalty was the result of Haiti being divided under two military generals in 1806. After the death of Toussaint L'Ouverture, General Henri Christophe became the ruler of the northern part and General Alexander Petion ruled in the western and southern area. Mini Sheller argues that "north-south split of the country... represented a regional, class and racial fault-line within the ruling groups, which destabilized attempts to unify the island. The mulatto landowning elites in the south and the new black generals, especially in the north, fostered color divisions within the elite and undermined class solidarity."[247]

A second problem that has condemned the Haitian masses to almost two centuries of illiteracy, poverty and hopelessness is related to the historic entrenched power of the military. The Haitian masses fought and won their struggle for emancipation from the centuries old burden of slavery. They understood their fight for independence as an opportunity to own small plots of land. They even succeeded in creating an independent government with a constitution modeled after the Constitution of the French Republic. But Article Nine of that constitution, written by Toussaint L'Ouverture, declared that "No one is worthy of being a Haitian if he is not a good father, a good son, a good husband, and above all a good soldier."[248]

That same constitution envisioned "a fraternal brotherhood-in-arms of all men of African descent" basic to nation building. Serving in the military was viewed as a high national calling. All during the years of their struggle to overcome slavery, the masses regarded their military leaders as national heroes. It was easy, therefore, for military symbolism to continue to be transposed into national leadership. In fact, says Sheller, "Military republicanism, which initially served the necessary purpose of building a new state . . . soon became the raison d'etre . . . (the reason or justification for existence)...for a state in which there were few civil institutions to balance an overwhelmingly military power."[249]

The Haitian political leaders who survived were those who successfully forged alliances with the generals. In Haiti, the road to power and land ownership in the nineteenth century republic was to be a military person. Landowning generals quickly dominated the governments of Haiti in both the north and south and eventually, in the united nation. Those political aspirants who were not of the military served as President or held other offices because they were selected and supported by the Haitian generals and the armed forces. "Haiti's initial decades of war-torn state-formation thus tended toward what has been described as "a republic monarchy sustained by the bayonet."[250] There is a Haitian proverb that says, "Constitutions are paper, bayonets are iron." That was an apt description of Haiti in 1823.

Although Jean-Pierre Boyer was President when the Reverend Thomas Paul arrived at Cap Haitian, he had been appointed by the generals. Paul spent a month distributing bibles and tracts and then traveled to Port-au-Prince, the nation's capital city. He traveled for three days over poor roads, escorted by personal guards to protect him from roving bands of bandits and former Haitian soldiers. When he arrived in Port-au-Prince, he was received by President Boyer. The Baptist missionary presented letters of introduction and the special Bible from the American Bible Society and was assured that he would be free to preach without restrictions of any kind. President Boyer's only words of caution were to encourage Paul to be careful since he would be preaching to many who were illiterate and whose lives were highly influenced by Voodoo priests. For most of the Haitians Paul would encounter, it would be their first exposure to Christian preaching and teaching in general and Protestant Baptist Christianity in particular. The President assured Paul, however, that if he gently engaged and won the people's confidence, in years to come many houses of worship would be built and all would enjoy religious privileges as in the United States of America. Their meeting lasted for two hours.[251] Subsequently, Paul spoke to small groups in the capital city.

After a month, Paul returned to Cap Haitian with letters of introduction to General Magny, the military commander of the Region of the North. General Magny asked to be notified of Paul's first meeting held in a large rented room. When Paul wrote to the Massachusetts Baptist Missionary Society in Boston, he reported that approximately fifty people attended his first preaching service. During a prayer meeting held three days later, he discovered that there were eight or ten persons in attendance who were already immersed baptized believers. He did not explain the circumstances leading to their baptism although it could be assumed that they may have come under the influence of the Bahamian Baptist named Tredwell referred to earlier.

Paul scheduled his first Communion Service for the following Sunday. At times, during Bible Study and worship services, as many as 200 men, women and children were in attendance. On week days, Missionary Paul visited families, distributed Bibles and religious tracts. In their books, Charles Roman and Doctor Pressoir agree that the Baptist missionary may have been the first ordained Christian minister to administer baptism by immersion in Haiti.[252]

Paul's reports to the Massachusetts Baptist Missionary Society indicate that he was very encouraged and elated by the response of the Haitian people who attended his evangelistic efforts. The minutes of the Society for September 16, 1823, indicate that four letters had been received from Paul. He volunteered to remain in Haiti for an additional three months if the Society approved and extended his appointment. The Society, however, did not approve his request even though subsequent letters and reports from non-Baptist missionaries and Haitian officials praised Paul's evangelistic efforts among the people of Haiti.[253] No reasons for their action is mentioned in the minutes, although prior to Paul's trip to Haiti, the focus of the Baptists of Massachusetts and elsewhere had been expanding their missionary efforts in Burma, Liberia, among the American Indians and European-Americans who were living in sparsely areas of the western United States.

When Jean-Pierre Boyer visited Paul just before he returned to Boston, the President expressed personal sorrow, assuring the Baptist missionary that he had earned the trust of the governing officials and the people. He invited him to return to Haiti. When Paul returned to Boston he attempted to resume his pastoral duties at First African Baptist Church even though he was weakened and suffering from diseases contacted in Haiti. During the six months he had spent in Haiti, First African had been operating under the interim direction of several associate ministers, church officials and strong community leaders. One of the associate ministers had been Paul's son, Nathaniel.

It is believed that Paul became active in the struggle to abolish slavery and fight for the improvements of black people in general. It is believed that he and a lay theologian named David Walker were collaborators and supporters in the publishing of *Freedom's Journal*, edited by John B. Russworm and Samuel Cornish. In 1829, unable to regain his health, Paul resigned as pastor of the oldest independent black Baptist church in the north and left Boston to settle permanently in Haiti, probably with the intent to build on his previous efforts and develop an independent Christian mission ministry. Unfortunately, he never regained his health. At age fifty-eight, in 1831, Thomas Paul, the first African-American pioneer Baptist missionary to the first independent black nation in the Western Hemisphere died in the island country he had made his home.[254]

Five years after Paul's death, in a letter to the Massachusetts Baptist Missionary Society, a Bahamian minister named Reverend Bourn, reported that in northern Haiti, there was a group of Baptists numbering twenty to thirty people in Cap Haitian. Even without a pastor, they continued to meet occasionally.[255] Notwithstanding, it was not until ninety-one years had elapsed that the Society was moved to commission another Baptist clergyman for service in Haiti.[256] The decision not to follow up on Paul's initial effort may have been result of the unstable political problems posed by the changing leadership in Haiti, and the twin problems of illiteracy and language. The time had not arrived when missionary societies from North America and England would entrust the Christian missionary enterprise to native pastors and potential indigenous leadership.

In 1843, one of the first decisions of a newly-organized American Free Baptist Mission in Boston was to follow up on Thomas Paul's earlier effort. A Caucasian, the Reverend William Mead Jones was ordained for missionary service in Haiti. Seventy-five years later (1923), one of a group sent by the same mission group was an African-American named William Monroe. Two evangelism centers were established; one in the southern seacoast town of Jacmel and the other in Trou-du-nord, located about forty miles east of Cap Haitian. Moore became frustrated because of his inability to communicate and returned to the United States after only four months. Later he served as a Baptist Missionary in the English speaking West African country of Liberia.[257]

Notes

[247]Sheller, p. 59.
[248]Ibid., p. 53.
[249]Ibid.

[250]Ibid., p. 56.
[251]Pressoir, pp. 110, 111; Romain, p. 58.
[252]Ibid., pp. 110-115 and p. 58.
[253]Minutes of the Massachusetts Baptist Missionary Society located in the Historical Documents Department on lower level of Franklin Trask Library, Andover Newton School of Theology at Newton Centre, Massachusetts.
[254]Horton and Horton, p. 100.
[255]Pressoir, p. 114.
[256]Romain, p. 59.
[257]Ibid., p. 7.

Chapter Twenty-Three

MISSIONARIES FROM ENGLAND AND JAMAICA

British Missionary Efforts: A Continuing Dilemma

The often selfless Christian leadership of the Baptist missionaries from England that supported and advanced the efforts of George Liele and Moses Baker in Jamaica was extended to Haiti. A viable mission effort by the British Missionary Society was vigorously promoted by William Knibb, founder and pastor of the First Baptist Church of Falmouth (Trelawny Parish) in Jamaica. In a few short years, Knibb had been arrested and jailed, charged for inciting the slaves to rebel in the 1832 Christmas Wars. Exiled to England, he became an avid emotional leader in the political struggle that resulted in the abolition of slavery and the emancipation of slaves in England and other British colonies. For many years, Knibb and several other English Baptist ministers in Jamaica were persistent in their effort to have the British Missionary Society extend its mission emphasis to the island of Haiti.

Their efforts were rewarded. Unfortunately, Knibb died thirteen days (November 15, 1845) after the first British mission outpost was established at Jacmel on November 3, 1845. The first English missionaries were the Reverend E. H. Francis and his wife who had previously served in Jamaica. They were the first of many men and women who made up the efficient evangelization teams that contributed to integrating the Christian faith into the lives of thousands of Haitians. Most of the missionaries were stricken by tropical diseases and died in Haiti or returned to Jamaica or England. Nevertheless, their mission tree continued to sprout and bear fruit for almost forty years.[258]

Missionary Francis organized the first mission school in Jacmel. In addition to evangelizing efforts, Francis, as did the pioneer African-American George Liele, believed that an effective gospel ministry was inextricably dependent on Christian and secular education. The missionaries began first with a Sunday school. The children of well-to-do Haitians did not seem to appreciate it. Children of the lower class wanted to attend the school but did not because they didn't have clothes to wear. The missionaries begged friends in England to send clothing. In April 1846, the first weekly elementary and middle school in Haiti opened. Boys and girls were separated and attended classes in separate buildings. When Francis requested the assistance of a native (Jamaican) instructor, a member of First Baptist, Falmouth, responded. She was an African-Jamaican teenager named Ms. Clarke who had spent three years with the Francis family.[259]

The first Baptist chapel was constructed and the concept of providing classical education as a basis for successful Christian evangelism was introduced in 1849 by another missionary, the Reverend W.H. Webley. In 1880, the energetic Reverend Alexandre Von Papenhoffen (a.k.a. Papingouth) reorganized the membership and repaired buildings partially destroyed during periods of civil war, political strife that included violent attacks from hostile Voodoo groups. Periods of civil unrest, political strife and Voodoo hostilities interrupted church worship and resulted in mission schools suspending classes. One profound aspect of Papenhoffen's ministry that led to the advancement of Christian evangelism and Baptist Church growth in Southern Haiti was his ability to win the hearts of young Haitians to Christ. One young Haitian, Nosirel L'herrison, had been educated in France. His parents were socially prominent Roman Catholics and yet, in a public service, L'herrison was baptized on December 22, 1885. Ten years later, he became the very influential independent Haitian pastor of the First Baptist Church of Jacmel.

In spite of the steady growth and development of their mission effort at Jacmel, the British Missionary Society's primary focus continued to be in areas of the world other than the

Caribbean, primarily Burma and West Africa. Two factors were influential in the Society's decision to completely discontinue its efforts in Haiti. First, was the continuous disruptions caused by ongoing political instability, civil wars, and massacres which resulted in the mission center being abandoned and the missionaries removed for reasons of safety. Second, the Society approved the request of the British missionaries and African-Jamaican church leadership to become self-supporting and autonomous. Once that was achieved, negotiations began to transfer operational and financial support for the mission center in southern Haiti to British and African-Jamaican Baptists under the umbrella of the newly formed Jamaican Baptist Union. Providentially, William Knibb had also been an organizing force leading to Jamaican Baptists becoming self-supporting. From its inception, the Union was committed to sponsor "a mission to West Africa and programs to other West Indies islands" including Haiti.[260]

Afro-Jamaicans: Mission Recipients Become Missionaries

An Afro-Jamaican minister named George H. Rowe was the first of two missionaries sent to Haiti from the Jamaica/Kingston Mission Society. It was his second mission tour. His first experience in Haiti, from 1876 to 1880, as a young inexperienced missionary under the supervision of the British Missionary Society, was very brief, ending when he was replaced by Alexander Von Papenhoffen. And then, in 1886, he replaced Von Papenhoffen at Jacmel. The Haitian historian, Romain, credits a more mature Rowe as being one of the founders of the Jacmel Baptist Church.[261] When he arrived for his second tour of missionary service, he was under the auspices of the Jamaican Mission Society, symbolizing the official ending of British Missionary Society involvement and responsibility for Baptist missions in Haiti.

Rowes' return to Haiti under Jamaican sponsorship represented a continuation of the African-American Baptist gospel thread that began when George Liele left colonial Georgia and established the first Baptist witness in Jamaica a little over a century previously. In addition, Rowe probably did not know that two-former slaves from British North America, Liele and Moses Baker, were the ones who invited the British Missionary Society to commit its resources to assist two pioneer Baptist preachers in Jamaica. There he was, another man of color, extending the black Baptist gospel thread to Haiti. George Lowe as the first ordained black Baptist minister/missionary sponsored by the majority Afro-Jamaican mission group was a spiritual descendant of George Liele and Moses Baker. Under the leadership of Rowe and others who followed him, Baptist missions and the Christian presence would expand in all parts of Haiti. Only the lack of missionary personnel, financial support from Jamaica and resulting organizational inefficiency combined with the lack of an aggressive program resulted in marginal successes compared to what could have been realized.[262]

Nonetheless, two aspects of Rowe's productive tour of duty at Jacmel and the south-eastern area of Haiti should be noted. Under Rowe's leadership, mission services and church school efforts became more regular and constant. In addition, a member of the mission church, a Haitian schoolteacher and poet, Nosirel L'herrison, taught Rowe to converse in the French language. Using French to communicate with the people in the Jacmel area, he revived an evangelistic effort that focused on the village of Arregy in an area strongly influenced by two Vodun societies. That in itself was an audacious effort. Just two years previously, the later part of 1884, violence, initiated and sustained by Vodun priests and their followers who lived in the mountain areas around Jacmel, left eleven people dead. British and other Christian missionaries were terrorized. Efforts to evangelize the peasants had been abandoned. L'herrison proved to be a very creative and resourceful lay leader in Missionary Rowe's planned evangelistic effort.[263] When Rowe returned to Jamaica, he left the Jacmel church under the supervision of its lay leaders, the most effective and influential being L'herrison.

The Reverend L. Tom Evans (a.k.a. Tom Evans), the second Jamaican missionary and Rowe's successor arrived from Kingston in 1889. He found that L'herrison had established a unifying and harmonizing presence throughout the congregation, providing a sense of mission continuity.[264] Evans only spent two years at Jacmel but during that period, rebuilt the chapel and reopened the mission school. In 1893, he led the church to become self-supporting and autonomous, not requiring any financial assistance from foreign sources. A Haitian minister, Lucius Hyppolite, who will be discussed later, encouraged Evans and the church membership to become a "Strict" Baptist Church, reflecting strong emphasis on the Biblical teaching of monogamous single family relationships, believers baptism, church organization and keeping Baptist/Christian ordinances and services free of all neo-African (especially Voodoo) beliefs and ceremonies.[265]

During the same year, Evans agreed with the recommendation of the officers and members of the independent church that Nosirel L'herrison be ordained as their permanent pastor. Under L'herrison's leadership, the church expanded. Its success stimulated financial support from the Jamaican Baptist Union, British missionaries in Jamaica and the newly organized African-American Lott Carey Missionary Baptist Convention.[266]

The Afro-Jamaican, Tom Evans, was the first person to recognize that the continuance and development of Baptist missions in Haiti were severely handicapped and jeopardized by the lack of personnel and financial support from churches in Jamaica. He took it upon himself to seek help from Lott Carey. That decision was very important in maintaining Jamaican Baptist mission efforts. The Lott Carey Convention accepted total responsibility for the mission churches in the St. Marc area and engaged the Reverend Evans to act as Area General Superintendent.[267] Evans also sought to interest the American Baptist Home Mission Society (ABHMS). His thorough knowledge of the scope and condition of Baptist missions throughout Haiti was a deciding factor in the ABHMS decision to re-evaluate the reports of Thomas Paul (1823) and investigate the possibilities for a meaningful mission endeavor.

Neither Dr. C.S. Brown or Dr. A.M. Moore who were sent to Haiti as the investigatory committee that recommended supporting missions were probably knowledgeable about George Liele,

George Baker, Prince Williams and Thomas Paul. Their report to the Lott Carey Missionary Society probably did not commit themselves to become continuing participants in the work of strengthening the Black Christian gospel thread that connected Georgia, Massachusetts, and Spanish East Florida with Jamaica, Bahama Islands and Haiti. They most likely would have been amazed and perhaps shocked to learn that before the missionary whose name they carried proudly reached West Africa in 1821, George Liele, initially unsupported by any church group, had been in Jamaica thirty-nine years.

Notes

[258] Pressoir, pp. 94, 138, 139.
[259] Romain, p. 6.
[260] Payne, pp. 30, 31.
[261] Romain, p. 61.
[262] Ibid., p. 62.
[263] Pressoir, p. 166.
[264] Romain, p. 62.
[265] Pressoir, p. 167.
[266] Pressoir, p. 166; Romain, pg 62.
[267] Pressoir, p. 94.

Chapter Twenty-Four

HAITIAN BAPTIST PIONEERS AND CHURCH BUILDERS

The Hyppolite Legacy: Independent Haitian Baptist Churches

An American missionary, the Reverend William L. Judd, had served as a pastor of a Baptist church in Meredith, New York for seven years prior to arriving in Haiti in 1847. Most of his twenty years as a missionary were spent in Port-au-Prince. One of the people converted and baptized under his pastorate was a Haitian named Sadrac Hyppolite.[268] Some years later, Judd was forced to leave Haiti suddenly because of political turmoil. Without a Baptist replacement, the congregation turned to a Methodist minister named Byrd. Hyppolite, a man of considerable influence and material substance, wanted to remain a Baptist. He replaced Byrd as the church's leader, found another group of Baptist Christians in Port-au-Prince and encouraged them to join his independent church. While there is no evidence that he was ever ordained as a Christian minister, over a period of time, he used his influence and finances to purchase property and construct a church house which opened in 1885. He gave the church edifice to the congregation in 1890. He also used his resources to open an evangelization center and build a school, probably for the children of the wealthy elite ruling class.[269]

Meanwhile, he sent his son, Lucius, to the United States to prepare for the Christian ministry. Ten years of study began at Madison College (Brooklyn, New York) and, in 1886, he graduated from Andover Newton Theological Institute (now Theological School) in Boston (Newton Centre), Massachusetts. That institu-

First Baptist Church, Port-au-Prince.

tion is considered to be the oldest Baptist seminary in the United States. It is located just a few miles east the Boston Commons and First African (or Joy Street) Baptist Church organized by Thomas Paul. As was expected of socially prominent Haitians of his day, Lucius Hyppolite also studied in France. Eventually, he also studied for one year at Calabar School of Theology in Jamaica, the school founded by the British Missionary Society for the preparation of ministers and teachers for church service.[270]

Lucius Hyppolite returned to Haiti in 1890. Before committing himself to a "father-influenced pastorate" at the church his father had built, he decided to establish his own ministerial portfolio. He served in a variety of pastoral and administrative areas of Christian Ministry among which was General Superintendent of the Lott Carey Convention sponsored Baptist Mission group of churches in St. Marc, Cap Haitian and Jacmel. In this role, he succeeded the Reverend Tom Evans. Leroy Fitts, in his critically acclaimed book on the life of Lott Carey and the Lott Carey Convention movement, lists Hyppolite and Evans as two of "The pioneers of the Convention's Haitian missionary projects. . . ."[271] In his role of General Superintendent, Hyppolite visited all of the Baptist churches of Northern Haiti. He encouraged Nosirel L'herisson, pastor of the Baptist church in Jacmel, to study for the ministry. More than any other pastor or missionary, Hyppolite was responsible for waging a campaign mainly in rural areas of Haiti to cleanse Baptist churches of all non-Baptistic and Voodoo influenced practices, theology and ceremonies. He focused on churches that had been founded or serviced by missionary leadership from England, Jamaica or the United States. Those churches, like the church at Jacmel, became known as Strict Baptists.[272]

After five years on his own, Lucius Hyppolite became the pastor of First Baptist Church in Port-au-Prince and immediately embarked on an aggressive program to introduce and implement contemporary programs and ministries. He did not accept a salary from the church but supported himself and his family by serving as the principal of the school founded by his father. First Baptist was the first church in Haiti to have a library. Hyppolite also founded a Society of Religious Propaganda and received and distributed hundreds of Christian song books, bibles and religious tracts. He also accepted subsidies from the Jamaican Missionary Baptist Churches and Lott Carey Missionary Baptist Convention. The many changes and modifications of the church's ministries, programs and his son's contemporary vision were opposed by Sadrac Hyppolite, who was more traditional and conservative having been exposed to the ministries of British and Jamaican missionaries. The tension that developed between father and son may have been one of the reasons the First Baptist Church membership did not exceed fifty in number. However, after his father died in 1906, church growth did occur.

The occupation of Haiti, in 1915, by the United States Marines based on the grounds of humanitarian intervention under the doctrine of the Monroe Doctrine, was at all times, a controversial act both in and beyond Haiti. The Reverend Hyppolite, as did many Haitians, believed that the marines and other occupation officials were really there to protect investments and interests of the government and citizens of the United States, especially the approaches to the Panama Canal.[273] He did not live to see the withdrawal of the United States military presence. In spite of the handicap brought about by loss of eye sight, when Lucius Hyppolite died in 1927, the church membership numbered several hundred with mission churches in the rural areas of Riviere Froide and Malanga Mountain.[274]

Contributions of Elie and Reuben Marc

Many missionaries went to Haiti supported by a church or group of individuals. One of those of that genre whose labors had unusual impact on the expansion of missions in that country was Ms. Jemima Straight. Ms. Straight arrived in Haiti in 1880 with only the support of one member of the Nicetown Baptist Church near Philadelphia, Pennsylvania. She had a modest house built in the little village of St. Suzanne about fourteen miles east of Cap Haitian in northern Haiti. It became her evangelistic and teaching mission center. As she grew older, she began to publish articles about Haiti for religious newspapers. She also visited churches and seminaries in the United States, pleading for someone to join her as a missionary. One of those who was emotionally moved when he heard her presentation was a young man named Elie Marc.

Elie Marc had been born in France and was a student at Andover Newton Theological Institute. When he graduated in 1894, he left Boston with Ms. Straight to begin his ministerial career in Haiti. When she died, Marc continued, enlarged and expanded the mission ministries she had begun at St. Suzanne. In time, he also became the pastor of a small Baptist congregation organized by the Afro-Jamaican Baptist missionary, L. Tom Evans some years before, located at Trou-du-Norde, about six miles east of St. Suzanne. Marc also carried on extensive evangelistic and preaching missions. As a testimony of his efforts, some have called Elie Marc "the father of twentieth century Haitian Baptist Churches."[275]

When Marc became a citizen of Haiti, he married a young Haitian woman with whom he fathered six children. He supported his family and mission ministries by operating a small trading store. For more than fifty years, he labored for Jesus Christ among the people and amid the poverty and Voodoo influenced areas of northern and central Haiti. One of his sons, George, became a leading educator. Another, Reuben, became the pastor of the largest Protestant congregation in Haiti.[276]

In 1929, the Reverend Reuben Marc became the pastor of First Baptist Church in Port-au-Prince, succeeding Lucius Hyppolite. Like his father, Reuben was a graduate of Andover Newton Theological School (class of 1928) and was well prepared for a role as a leading pastor in his country. From the beginning, and for more than fifty years, the ministries and missions of the church under Marc's leadership were supported in various degrees, by the American Baptist Foreign Mission Society, later called the Board of International Missions, American Baptist Churches, USA.

Reuben Marc Remembered

For more than twenty years, as the pastor of the Macedonia Baptist Church, Pittsburgh, Pennsylvania and First Baptist Church Piney Grove, Fort Lauderdale, Florida, this writer traveled to Haiti two or three times a year (from 1974 to 1994) to inspect a variety of church mission ministries that included a nutrition center for children and an elementary school accommodating five hundred students in rural Metivier where several trails converged at a natural spring used by the people living in the area as a source of water, and a medical clinic and pharmacy for children and adults in the suburban area of Petionville called Bourg Champagne. I frequently worshiped at the eleven o'clock service at First Baptist Church in Port-au-Prince. Pastor Reuben Marc and this writer became friends because of our mutual affiliation with the American Baptist Churches, USA. On several occasions I was privileged to preach to the over-flow congregations assembled for worship on Sunday mornings. My sermon efforts, delivered in English, were always translated into French and Creole. In turn, Pastor Marc would always ask me to mail a large cache of letters when I returned to the United States to expedite and ensure delivery.

When questioned about the number of church members, seating capacity, ministries and missions, the Reverend Marc would say that the church membership numbered about eleven thousand. While many of them were educated elitists, political leaders and Haitian professionals, the overwhelming majority were the aspiring poor and less educated folk of Port-au-Prince. First Baptist Church, with the financial assistance of the Board of International Ministries, ABC, sponsored seventy-two satellite mission churches and schools in metropolitan Port-au-Prince and nearby rural areas.

Notes

[268] Romain, p. 59.
[269] Pressoir, p. 17.
[270] Ibid., p. 128.
[271] Leroy Fitts, *Lott Carey, First Black Missionary to Africa* (Valley Forge: Judson Press, 1978), p. 122.
[272] Pressoir, p. 129.
[273] From personal conversations with the Reverend Reuben Marc in January, 1979-1980, in Port-au-Prince, Haiti.
[274] Pressoir, p. 130.
[275] Romain, p. 71; Payne, p. 467.
[276] Romain, p. 72.

Chapter Twenty-Five

HAITIAN MISSION EFFORTS BY BAPTISTS FROM THE UNITED STATES

The Lott Carey Baptist Missionary Convention

Eighty-four years after Reverend Thomas Paul's historic mission inspection visit, the African-American Lott Carey Baptist Missionary Convention, in 1916, committed itself to establish and maintain a mission presence in Haiti. That commitment was in response to the request of the Afro-Jamaican missionary, L. Tom Evans, to support ongoing mission churches and schools established in Haiti by the Jamaican Missionary Society and the Jamaican Baptist Union. In his 1917 Annual Report, the Corresponding Secretary of the Lott Carey Convention noted, "In 1916 the Convention began work in Haiti in cooperation with Baptist pastors and private school teachers who were supplementing their small salaries by doing mission work on the island. The pioneers of the Convention's Haitian mission projects were Rev. Lucius Hyppolite, pastor and teacher in Port-au-Prince; Rev. James Jacques, the only Baptist pastor in Cap Haitian; Rev. Delfort Eustache, pastor of several churches in North Haiti; Rev. De Lattree in St. Marc; . . . the Rev. Tom Evans . . . and several others. . . ."[277]

Later, in 1925, the mission convention President, Rev. C. S. Brown, declared that because the two and one half million people of the only Negro republic in the Western World were inclined to be Baptist, the Lott Carey Convention was not only committed to evangelization and education, but "deeply interested in the political as well as the spiritual welfare of Haiti."[278] His words reflected the optimistic assumption of the African-American pastors and laity of the mission group that the only "door of hope for the Haitian people" was dependent on Lott Carey's commitment to reach all classes of that nation's society with Baptist doctrine and democratic principles.[279] Obviously, neither the President or the Lott Carey pastors present were knowledgeable of the social, political and military history of Haiti; therefore, their assumptions were unrealistic. Even with the help of the American Baptist Home Mission Society, many independent Baptist mission groups and even the goodwill, from time-to-time of strong political Haitian leaders such as President-for-Life Francois Duvalier (1957 to 1971), the Lott Carey Convention never had the money, personnel resources or knowledge of the nation to make a major difference, socially, educationally, politically or religiously in Haiti. Doubtless, many thousands of poor and aspiring Haitians were exposed to Christianity, converted, educated and their lives changed for the better because of the commitment and sacrifices of Lott Carey missionaries and teachers, especially in areas such as St. Marc in the northwest, Fonds-des- Negres in the southern region or the fourteen mission stations and worship center that seated 1,000 on the Island of Gonave. In many respects the mission efforts of the Lott Carey Missionary Convention were fruitful and beneficial.

Unfortunately, the changing political climates that produced nationwide unrest and instability when rulers such as "Pappa Doc" Duvalier died and others achieved power, the implacable problems, often barriers of language and missionaries susceptibility to various illnesses related to polluted water and diseases combined to present problems which, over a period of years, contributed to a reversal of the Convention's earlier successes. Acting on the recommendation of an investigative committee, the Lott Carey missionary presence in the Republic of Haiti was consummated on October 23, 1975, ending fifty-nine years of responsible mission leadership by a predominant African-American Baptist church group. However, a few years ago a Lott Carey sponsored mission was resumed in Haiti. Others continue on the African countinent in Liberia, Nigeria, Zaire, and South Africa and in India, Guyana, and Russia.

American Baptist Churches (USA): In the Footsteps of Thomas Paul

Prior to 1923, the primary mission foci of the American Baptist Home Mission Society were in Burma (Southern Asia), Liberia (West Africa), among Native Americans and planting and assisting Baptist churches in sparsely settled regions of the United States. The ABHMS also funded mission efforts such as those operated by the Jamaican Baptists and Lott Carey. However, in October 1923, exactly ninety years after Thomas Paul's six month mission feasibility experience in 1832, the first commissioned American Baptist missionary, the Reverend Arthur Groves Wood, arrived in Jacmel. He was welcomed by the Haitian, Nosirel L'herisson, pastor of the Jacmel (Strict) Baptist Church.[280]

For one year, Missionary Wood traveled throughout Haiti. He became familiar with the ministries of Elie Marc and the Jamaican Baptists. He also discovered that many Haitians who had converted to Christianity were still meeting and worshiping as Baptists without pastoral leadership. Using Cap Haitian as his base of mission operations, Wood labored to reorganize and strengthen all pioneer efforts. He also organized additional mission centers. All of the Baptist work was united and consolidated. Many Haitian (Native) pastors, including Elie Marc, became affiliated and were supported in whole or in part by the American Baptist Home Mission Society.[281]

The C. S. Kelleys, Afro-Jamaican Missionaries

A Jamaican, C.S. Kelly, accompanied by his wife, Mae, arrived in Haiti in 1938. Kelley was a businessman who had graduated from Calabar College. He had also studied at the Baptist Missionary Training College at Norwood, England, which specifically trained men and women to serve as foreign missionaries. His wife, the daughter of British missionaries, always wanted to follow in her parents' footsteps. She, too, had studied at the Missionary Training College. Initially, Kelly was the pastor of a mission church with the status of an ordinary native worker. Six years later, in 1944, he was commissioned as a missionary of the American Baptist Home Mission Society and placed in charge of two churches. One church located at Hinche, had a membership of about one thousand. The other, located at Trou-du-Nord, was a church established by Jamaican Baptist missionaries many years previously. It was also the church the resolute French-born Elie Marc had served as pastor for fifty years.

The Haitian people Kelly encountered seem to have quickly recognized that he, perhaps because of his Jamaican heritage, identified with their condition, hopes and aspirations, spiritually and emotionally just as the African-American Baptist pioneer and church founder, George Liele, had done in Jamaica. Of course, the Haitian Baptists were not aware when they enthusiastically endorsed Kelly's promotion in 1946 to succeed A.G. Wood as General Superintendent, that the Jamaican was extending the Baptist gospel thread that connected colonial North America with Jamaica and Haiti. As General Superintendent (a title inherited from the British and Jamaican mission groups) Charles Stanford Kelley's responsibility was to coordinate all mission personnel and all aspects of all American Baptist and former Jamaican Baptist missions. He not only preached and taught at every Baptist mission in Haiti but he was the spokesman for American Baptists on the national level.

The Haitian Baptist Convention

Kelley's leadership was a major contributing factor in 1964 and 1965 in helping the Haitian pastors and churches organize into a covenant association. A young Haitian pastor, a graduate of the American Baptist Seminary at Limbe in North Haiti whose name was Sem Marseille, provided the initiative and dynamism for the first Haitian Baptist attempt to unify. Marseille, along with Luc Nerre and Jules Thomas were undoubtedly familiar with the problems that had previously led to the failure of the l'Union Baptist d'Haiti (the Baptist Union of Haiti) because the many autonomous church groups and the number of inexperienced and untrained pastors could not agree for long around a central issue of designated leadership, even after struggling twenty-one years (1939 to 1960). General Superintendent Kelley's influence, the respect that all of the Haitian pastors had for him, proved to be the decisive factor that brought a covenant attempt into fruition as the Haitian Baptist Convention. The Reverend Sem Marseille was elected as the first president. A national headquarters was established in Cap Haitian, staffed by Haitians. Kelley not only served on the founding committee as its treasurer but continued to serve the Convention in an advisory role, representing the American Baptist Home Mission Society. He was especially gifted in helping the Haitian pastors and Convention leadership reach the level of maturity necessary to assume decision making responsibilities and administrative leadership. The Reverend Marseille became the Executive Director of La Maison Biblique (Bible House), known throughout the Caribbean and Latin America as the equivalent of the American Bible Society.[282]

Contemporary Missions Supported by American Baptist Churches, USA

In 1947, the American Baptists sent the Reverend Harold K. Heneise, his wife and three children to Haiti. The Heneises formed a formidable dedicated teaching and administrative team. Together they founded the Haitian Baptist Theological Seminary at Limbe where thousands of Haitian men and women have been educated and prepared for Christian ministry. The seminary continues training pastors and church workers for churches in Haiti and the United States. Many of the seminary's graduates have migrated to the United States and have planted dozens of churches as the Haitian immigrant population increases.[283] In the same Cap Haitian locale, American Baptist missionaries have also founded the Christian University Northern Haiti and the Good Samaritan Hospital at Limbe that during 1987 treated over 100,000 patients in the clinic. Many of them travel for many miles and spend days and nights waiting in the hospital courtyard for medical treatment.

The Baptist Agricultural Center at Quartier Morin has projects to educate Haitian farmers and agriculture workers and to plant trees and seedlings which are distributed to farmers to plant to aid soil quality and provide firewood and charcoal. Also, animals, such as rabbits, pigs, and chickens are being raised to enlarge the food supply for the Haitian people. In Cap Haitian, the Haitian Baptist Convention operates a youth center that provides job training for young people while another center offers music, recreation and Bible study. The denomination also operates an optical center. In 1992, based on a recommendation by a mission inspection tour group led by this writer, the American Baptist Churches of the South (a region of ABC/USA) sent over 3,500 pairs of used/castoff eye glasses collected from American Baptist churches to the optical center to be distributed as needed. Several churches from Georgia, the state in which the African-American Baptist preacher George Liele received his spiritual vision to go to Jamaica and share the Good News of Jesus Christ to slaves and free persons as the first Baptist Christian Missionary, participated in the used/castoff eye glasses project.

Notes

[277] Leroy Fitts, *The Lott Carey Legacy of African American Missions* (Baltimore: Gateway Press, 1993), p. 99.
[278] *The Lott Caarey Herald*, Vol 18, September, 1925), p. 155.
[279] Fitts, p. 101.
[280] Romain, p. 72.
[281] Romain, pp. 72, 73; Fitts, p. 99.
[282] Romain, pp. 74, 79.
[283] Ibid, p. 74.

Chapter Twenty-Six

WHY BAPTISTS AND OTHER PROTESTANTS HAVE NOT IMPACTED HAITI
(AS IN JAMAICA AND THE BAHAMA ISLANDS)

Vodun: A Formidable Neo-African Religion

One reason why Baptists and other foreign and Native Protestant denominational missionaries, church leaders and teachers have been unable to impact Haiti as they have in Jamaica and the Bahama Islands is the continued strength of Vodun. One hundred and twenty-nine years after the first Baptist missionary, Reverend Thomas Paul, began preaching in Cap-Haitian (1823 to 1952), the Haitian Department of Cults reported that (in 1952) there were approximately (322,550 Protestant Christians in Haiti. Of that number, 177,148 were members of six different Baptist church groups.[284] These statistics which are numerical estimates, suggest that at that time, more than one-half of all Protestant Christians in that predominantly Afro-Haitian nation were Baptists. Since then, there has been a remarkable gain in the growth of Pentecostal churches, such as the Church of God in Christ, but Baptists may still make-up the largest Protestant group.

Nevertheless, there are those who say that "For better or for worse, Haiti is a magic island, and the laughter of a thousand gods echoes through her hills....Voodoo continues alive and well in Haiti. . . ."[285] Especially Haitians who live in rural areas and peasants who claim to be Roman Catholics, may regularly offer sacrifices to the loa, are possessed by them, and every Saturday night respond to the throbbing rhythm of the drums, but sincerely think of themselves as good Catholics. They faithfully receive communion and contribute to their churches and the salaries of their priests. There are few signs of improvement. The Catholic Church's tolerance for this may be attributed to the attitude of the priests. Thirty years ago, it was reported, "when schools are beginning to multiply and peasants are no longer cut off in the mountains . . . when Catholic priests (who come mostly from Brittany in France) are confronted by parishioners who are visited by spirits...they are bewildered and helpless." On the other hand, as Alfred Metrauix argues, "in certain Protestant sects which abound in Haiti (Baptists, Pentecostalists, Methodists, Anglicans and Adventist) Voodoo has found . . . formidable and tenacious adversaries. . . ." Many members of these church groups, Metrauix continues, consider Voodoo (or Vodon) "Satanism" and treat it with total intransigence. Converts are required to break totally. On the other hand, many Catholics practice it more or less openly.[286]

There is little evidence that supports any claim that the Roman Catholic Church has ever been concerned about the personal development of the Haitian masses. In 1987, sixty-seven percent of the voting population elected a former Roman Catholic priest as President of Haiti whose sermons to his congregants was sprinkled by a vision of a "peoples church" and Liberation Theology. Jean-Bertrand Aristide succeeded Jean-Claude Duvalier also known as "Baby-Doc." Within a few months, he and his government was overthrown by a military junta recognized (and perhaps supported) by the Vatican (Roman Catholic Church government) and the Dominican Republic. In a strange way, history repeated itself. President Aristide writes, that just as it had happened many times in the history of the first independent Black controlled and governed nation in the Western Hemisphere, the Bishops (perhaps with the approval of the Pope) of the Roman Catholic Church allied with the Haitian military and the oligarchy made up of the rich and powerful 1 percent of the population, to overthrow Aristide and the Lavalas government. Assisted by foreign interests who distrusted government of the people, by the people and for the people, the groups whose goals for Haiti Aristide distrusted, were installed to rule Haiti again. "Through its Monsignor Baldisser, (the Apostolic Nuncio in Haiti) the Vatican government in Rome was the only diplomatic recognition the Haitian junto received."[287]

Metrauis believes the reason many Voodoo worshipers have been converted to Protestantism is because they saw and still see in the Baptist or other denominations a refuge. There is a Haitian saying, "If you want the loa to leave you in peace—become a Protestant."[288]

It is difficult to measure the influence of some missionaries and teachers, especially the Baptists, but unquestionably the establishment of schools for the rural population and offering adults the opportunity to learn to read and write have contributed to the growth and impact of some Protestant denominations such as the Baptists. When entire families of prominent people are among Protestant church worshipers, examples of Haitians liberated from the terrorism of Vodun is lifted up for the rural peasants to evaluate and emulate.

And then, says Metrauix, "there is an economic aspect, too, which is not without importance. . . . (Some people) . . . are sometimes tempted to believe that they have only to become Protestant to improve their lot. . . . (He argues further that . . . Baptists (especially) make fewer demands on their members than do Catholicism and Voodoo. . . . (For instance) . . . Peasants have to pay considerable sums for treatments which are almost magical. . . . From a strictly economic point of view it is undeniable that Voodoo heavily burdens the resources of the peasant population. . . . As long as there is no organized medical service in Haiti voodoo will go on."[289]

The Reverend J. Van Alfred Winsett, his wife, Jacquelyn, and five other adult members of a mission evangelistic group from the Ebenezer Baptist Church of Pittsburgh, Pennsylvania, still shudder when they speak about the terrifying night they experienced in a mountainous rural area of Haiti approximately eighteen years ago (1985). They had traveled to Haiti to inspect their church-sponsored orphanage mission for children in Port-au-Prince, directed by one of the Ebenezer members, the Reverend Shirley Pierre. They were told that there was a village called Fondurec in the mountainous high rural area, where the people had never been exposed to Christianity of any kind. Deciding to preach and witness in that village, Pastor Winsett and others negotiated with a man to drive them to the village in his truck.

Three and one-half hours later, as the group neared the mountain area late in the afternoon, but still miles short of their destination, the driver stopped the truck near a little village and demanded more money. The Ebenezer Evangelistic Team refused, citing the agreement made previously. The driver ordered them to get off his truck and drove away. He returned several times, as they stood beside the narrow dirt road, to ask if they were willing to meet his financial demands. Each time the group refused. Finally, as the evening shadows fell, he drove off and did not reappear, leaving the group to spend the night in the open air, planning to sleep on the ground.

A man who lived in the village, approached, and speaking Creole to the Reverend Pierre, offered his little shanty home for the night, advising them to lock the door. About midnight, as the seven of them, three men and four women, tried to settle down for the night in the small room, they heard drums and chanting, the sound growing louder as a group of people drew nearer. Deacon Briscoe wryly announced, "Here comes the welcome wagon." The group, men and women, waving lighted torches, boisterously encircled the small house and began beating on the door, windows and the outer tin veneer with heavy sticks, poles and rocks, yelling and screaming, as Shirley Pierre translated, "You're going to die tonight." It would be an understatement to say that the group was terrified, a terror that became horror as they contemplated the real possibility of being burned alive. They peeped through cracks of the house but all they could see beyond the crowd was the utter darkness of rural Haiti. They huddled together, trying to find comfort by singing hymns and prayed for deliverance.

After several hours, the noise diminished and abated as the crowd outside withdrew in one direction only to be replaced by another group who came from another direction a few minutes later. The process of intimidation and threatening resumed, except the second time, the noise level was higher. Again the loud drums beating with the larger group shouting and chanting raised the terror level of the small Baptist evangelistic group. No one slept inside the house. The harassment continued for several hours, until the light of dawn began to disperse the darkness, and then the second group melted away also.

As the sun rose, amid the silence of the dawn, the group, led by Pastor Winsett, emerged from the house to freshen themselves with the water of a creek flowing nearby. A solicitous village woman brought them food for breakfast—one egg and a sour grapefruit to be divided among seven adults. Finally, a group of people from the village of Fondurec, their original destination, appeared. Somehow, the villagers had received word that the Ebenezer Church group was in danger and had walked the miles from their homes to rescue their Christian guests. They informed the Ebenezer Church group that the man who had loaned the group his house was in reality a Voodoo priest (bocor, hounfort or houngan). Obviously, he had organized the terror campaign to discourage them from preaching the gospel and witnessing to the people in their village.

The group from Ebenezer Baptist Church decided to witness and preach anyhow, at the site of their fear, distress, duress and persecution. The Reverend Winsett preached, and the Reverend Pierre translated his sermon about Jesus into Creole. The Reverend Pierre, a native of Pittsburgh married to a Haitian, preached in Creole with her pastor and friends from Ebenezer providing prayerful and musical support. One boy from the village was converted and returned to his home to face the frenzy of the worshipers of Vodun, in the rural mountainous region of Haiti.[290]

A short time later, the Ebenezer evangelistic group hailed a man driving his truck loaded with grain to be sold at the markets in Port-au-Prince. He offered them a ride on top of the grain, which they gratefully accepted. They returned to the capital city, all seven weary but triumphant and happy Baptists, rejoicing on top of the truck for more than three hours. The "terror" of riding on the truck-top, down the narrow roads of Haiti, was almost a "joyride" compared to what they had experienced. In time, they may realize that, in their way, they were extending the invisible but undeniably religious-cultural gospel thread of Christianity that a Baptist preacher began when he arrived in Haiti from Boston about 150 years before.

The influence of Vodun or Voodoo, not only survives in the rural areas of Haiti but the struggle for the souls and lives of the peasants and city dwellers is still a priority concern for the Christian Church, just as it was for Thomas Paul and the others.

Vodun has again achieved national respect. In addition to permitting a voodoo priestess to bestow a presidential sash on him at his first inauguration in 1991, President Jean-Bertrand Aristide recently (April 2003) issued an executive decree inviting voodoo adherents and organizations to register with the Haitian Ministry of Religious Affairs. Practitioners of Vodun who swear an oath before a civil judge will then be able to legally conduct ceremonies such as marriages and baptisms. In spite of the fact that the Roman Catholic Church led a campaign in the 1940s to destroy all Vodun temples and sacred objects, the President of Haiti, a former Roman Catholic priest, has indicated that he recognizes voodoo as "an ancestral religion...an essential part of national identity," which "represent a considerable portion of Haiti's 8.3 million people."[291]

By no means is the practice and influence of Vodun confined to the island of Haiti. David Ovalle, writing in *The Miami Herald* recently, reported that South Florida law enforcement agencies have engaged anthropologists to teach week long courses on ritualistic religions. Police offices in Miami will learn about Cuban Santeria, West African Congo Palo Mayombe and Haitian Vodun to become knowledgeable about the religions they are encountering. Ovalle estimates that tens of thousands of practitioners of these religions have immigrated to South Florida. Haitian Vodun is considered more mysterious than the others because its ceremonies often include the use of machetes as props and magic powders. "Worshipers," says Ovalle, "often dress up as Baron Samedi, the deity of death. Followers will often dance to drums and wear dark clothing and top hats to honor the deity."[292]

In another article that appeared in the same newspaper, Jane Regan reported on a three-day holiday that, every year for the past 150 years has honored Our Lady of Mount Carmel, the patron saint of Ville Bonheur (Happy Village), and Erzuli, a Vodou spirit associated with water and sometimes also portrayed as the Virgin Mary. According to Regan, "Every July . . . rich, poor and middling Haitians have made the journey from around the country and abroad to the tiny village of Ville Bonheur and the nearby Saaut d'Eau waterfall, 60 miles north of Port-au-Prince . . . in 1847, . . . Our Lady of Mount Carmel is said to have appeared on a palm tree and begun to heal the sick. . . . (A) French Catholic priest cut down the tree, but worshipers still came. . . . Eventually the church bowed to the inevitable, erected a cross and built a church on the spot. . . . Inside the church . . . (every July). . . . Hundreds of believers—many wearing the variously colored belts and ropes of Vodou spirits—*offer candles and flowers as they crowd the altar, clutching passports or photos, crying and praying to a statue of the Virgin Mary.*" (Italics the writer)[293] According to Regan, "Vodou followers believe in one supreme God who has many spirit assistants, intermediaries between the supreme being and humans."[294] One of those present, in a bright swimsuit, was a sixteen-year-old teen-age girl from Sunrise, Florida.

Notes

[284]Pressoir, pp. 107, 108.
[285]Heinl and Heinl, p. 487.
[286]Alfred Metrauix, *Voodoo in Haiti* (Brooklyn: Schocken Books, Inc., 1972), pp. 323, 336, 352.
[287]Jean-Bertrand Aristide, *Dignity* (Charlottesville: University Press of Virginia, 1996), pp. 14, 19.
[288]Ibid., p. 352.
[289]Ibid., pp. 356-357, 363.
[290]As reported in a telephone conversation with Dr. J. Van Alfred Winsett on March 4, 2003, and subsequent personal meetings in Pittsburgh.
[291]Morton (the Star-Ledger)

[292]Ovalle, David. "Police Get Lessons On Exotic Religions," *Miami Herald*, 16 April, 2003, Broward Edition, 1B and 8B.

[293]Regan, Jane, "Haitians Seek Saint And Spirit," *Miami Herald*, 17 July, 2003, Broward Edition, pg. 3A.

[294]Ibid.

Chapter Twenty-Seven

UNPREDICTABLE SIGNS OF HOPE

Baptist Political Activism

One looks in vain for Afro-Haitian Baptist or other Protestant denominational political reformers or organizers who fought to extend responsible democratic government and citizen involvement to all, regardless of family connections, color or social and economic class. Over five centuries of political instability and military rule have combined to prevent the development of national religious and social revolutionaries such as the Afro-Jamaican Samuel (Daddy) Sharpe, William Gordon and Paul Bogle who are revered by school children and others as national heroes. There are at least four reasons for this.

First, while the people in the United States may not have known, Afro-Haitians have never forgotten that the United States military occupied Haiti for fifteen years (from 1919 to 1934). Even before placing Haiti under military rule, the U.S. Marines, in 1915, put down a revolt by Haitian peasants in favor of the Haitian elite, namely the wealthy light skin/white looking Mulattos and ever-present military generals. Four years later, in 1919, a leader of a (black) Haitian people's movement was actually assassinated with the permission, and some say, the actual involvement of the United States government as in Chile some years later during the presidency of Richard Nixon. Also, for twenty-nine years (1957 to 1986) President-for-Life, Francois Duvalier, and his son, Jean-Claude Duvalier, were given millions of dollars by the United States government that helped subsidize and maintain a brutal dictatorial system that promoted class difference, racial privileges for a few, and permitted a terrorizing judicial and prison system.[295]

Much is written and heard these days that the goal of the American government is to foster democratic governments and institutions all over the world, including the Middle Eastern nation of Iraq and Afghanistan in eastern Asia. And yet, according to Michael Heinl, "The Americans—reversing the cliche that the United States always tries 'to export democracy', laid no foundations, were really not allowed to lay foundations, for Haitians to rule themselves save in the old ways."[296] Years of occupation by the American military did not result in an effort to set in place the democratic institutions that are required to produce and insure a democracy that involves the education and political instruction necessary for the overwhelming black Haitian majority. In South Florida, thousands of Cubans gain citizen privileges and even citizenship almost every year because they claim to be escaping from a Communist ruled island. Haitian refugees, by contrast, are routinely returned or held in detention centers without any type of political indoctrination or education, until they can be returned to their country. Only two American Presidents, Jimmy Carter and William (Bill) Clinton, have directly interceded to challenge the military dictatorships of Haiti or protect leaders of social and political change from harassment and death.

Second, the dominance of the Haitian military or the many President-for-Life emperors who in fact have governed with dictatorial authority enforced by the military, police or secret terror gangs and thugs. In addition, the threat of United States brokered government assassinations have probably discouraged some efforts for the kinds of reforms that would eliminate the government inspired terror and death squads, street violence, physical abuse and imprisonment for organizing the masses to protest. When groups of Haitian citizens take to the streets to protest anything, they are contested in ways that usually lead to violence. That kind of intimidation can become a deterrent to anyone representing social, political or governmental reform.

Third, until recently, there was little evidence to indicate that since Haiti became an independent nation, neither the Roman

Catholic priests (since the days of Toussaint L'Ouverture) nor Protestant missionaries, including the Baptists, laid the foundation or planted seeds among those they instructed to contend for the Haitian masses. Nor did they attempt to inspire and develop visionary church leadership to contend for political change. Perhaps that was considered too dangerous. Walter B. Shurden in his highly recommended book, urges all Baptists to hold up and promote four historic fragile freedoms: freedom of the Bible, of the soul, of the church and of religion. However, one looks in vain for any word or phrase that portrays Baptists as promoters of individual, racial, ethnic, social, political freedom, freedom from fear, false imprisonment, racial or class prejudice, or the promotion of democratic institutions and justice.[297] The freedom to select which freedom to promote may be one reasons why Baptist missionaries from North America, Jamaica and England were willing to spend years suffering and dying from tropical diseases. They selected which freedoms they would preach and teach to promote spiritual salvation on strictly personal levels to the Haitian masses. To their credit, they provided basic educational opportunities to read the Bible to those they reached, but they may have encouraged the kinds of "spiritual" things which would not be threatening to the Haitian military and those leaders with absolute or dictatorial governmental authority. Interestingly, neither African American civil rights leaders, including the National Association for the Advancement of Colored People, the Southern Leadership Conference or the Congressional Black Caucus, have offered their services to the beleaguered people of Haiti. Like the missionaries, they, too, may have knowingly declined to encourage the kinds of stimulation of thought and vision that might have led to forms of resistance to the status quo.

Unfortunately, for the Haitian masses, there was no Haitian Native Baptist movement with its emphasis on African consciousness because the Neo-African movement known as Vodun (or Voodoo) was deeply rooted in magic and possession that did not have the world-vision of Myalism that surfaced in Jamaica. Had a type of Native Baptist Christianity developed, the military and dictatorship-type governments would not have permitted it to exist or, at minimum, would have encouraged severe harassment by the Vodun priesthood. Also, there was no Protestant religious group, like the Huguenots, whose pronouncements as Frenchmen may have given the leaders of the Haitian struggle for independence the motivation to adopt the great themes of the French Revolution: Liberty, Fraternity and Equality. As we have said, it has long been a mark of social distinction, elegance, and status for the children of mulatto and class-conscious well-to-do Haitians to study in France or marry into French families.

And yet, in spite of all the negatives listed above, Haitian Baptists are still the largest group of social and political activists in that island country. Some determined Haitians have placed their lives in danger to protest the status quo and organize the people to demand changes in the status quo. One of those persons was a Baptist preacher, the Reverend Luc Neree. In his book, Jean-Bertrand Aristide, reported that in 1976, Luc Neree, a Baptist pastor who was a political activist in Port-au-Prince, wrote a letter to President Jimmy Carter, informing him of the many abuses of human rights and other problems that Haitians, especially the poor and illiterate Afro-Haitians, were suffering from the government and military under Jean-Claude Duvalier. When Ambassador Andrew Young, a Christian clergyman, visited Haiti in August 1977, he spent his first night with Pastor Neree and his congregation at their church on Delmas Boulevard. The next day, the first rickety wooden sailboat with sixty-one people on board, sailed for the United States. They were the first "boat people."[298]

Later, probably feeling fairly secure because of the international publicity that resulted from Ambassador Young's visit, Neree wrote a letter criticizing a government cabinet official. He was set upon, beaten and left for dead by a band of Macoutes, Duvaliar's feared secret police. Somehow he survived and was brought to the United States on a private jet plane when President Jimmy Carter intervened on his behalf. According to Aristide, after narrowly escaping death, when Pastor Neree returned to Haiti, he "followed more closely his original vocation of minister/pastor of his flock."[299]

Another Baptist churchman who may still be a political activist if he has not been assassinated, is the Reverend Luc Musadieu, the pastor of a church in Gonaives, about forty miles northwest of Port-au-Prince. Musadieu dared to be a candidate for President and contended against Aristide. His home and his automobile were burned and the windows and other parts of his church building were damaged. Many Evangelical Christian ministers, however, are not involved in politics, preferring to provide a sense of comfort to their congregants, preaching sermons that stress holy living and preparation for life in the hereafter. One exception to that "play-it-safe" type of ministry has been a Bishop of the Church of God in Christ, Lopez Dautrauche.

The Reverend Sem Marseille, one of the organizers and the first president of the Haitian Baptist Convention, organized (in 1987) the President Electoral Council of Haiti, following the departure of "Baby Doc" Duvalier for "retirement" in France and Switzerland. The Council was composed of ministers of various Protestant church denominations (mostly Baptist), labor union leaders and university teachers. One of the concerns of the Council was the growing traffic in drugs through Haiti for sale in the United States, and the influence and power of drug dealers on the selection process for those who aspire to political office. Unfortunately, the group disbanded after only six months of activity. Since then, because of physical problems, the Reverend Marseille, a staunch American Baptist pastor, has found it necessary to leave Haiti and now lives near Orlando, Florida. His absence has left a void in independent leadership ranks. His quiet but honest and fearless qualities are not easily replaced. Marseille personified the highest moral and spiritual qualities of men like George Liele, Moses Baker, William Gordon, Prince Williams and others who helped forge the invisible and undeniably religious-cultural gospel thread of Christianity that connects African Americans with the descendants of African people living in Jamaica, The Bahamas, Haiti, and the Greater Caribbean Basin.

NOTES

[295]"Signs of Grace," *National Ministries*, American Baptist Churches (Valley Forge: November/December 1988), p. 35.

[296]Heinl, p. 475.

[297]Walter B. Shurden, *The Baptist Identity: Four Fragile Freedoms* (Macon, Georgia: Smyth and Helwys Publishing, Inc., 1993).

[298]Aristide, pp. 656, 660.

[299]Ibid., p. 663.

GLOSSARY

African Diaspora: the dispersals of population out of Sub-Sahara West Africa and Central Africa to be traded and sold into slavery in other parts of the world; for this book, the Western Hemisphere.

Anabaptists (ana = another (another baptism): an early sixteenth century movement evolving from Separatists who rejected infant baptism, requiring all members to be baptized or re-baptized by immersion. They emphasized the compatibility of human free will and Divine Sovereignty, and the role of God's unceasing love.

Baptists: A Christian Church denomination that started about 1610 in England, born out of the Separatist Movement which sought religious freedom from the Anglican Church, also known as the Church of England. The Baptists believed that the Bible was their sole authority, each church self-governing, and members joined by a voluntary covenant with Jesus Christ as head. The first Baptist church in North America was founded in 1689 by Roger Williams in Providence, Rhode Island for people seeking freedom of religious expression.

Convince: An ancestral cult that started in the easternmost areas of Jamaica.

Cumina: An ancestral cult in predominantly rural parts of Jamaica, probably descended from the religion of runaway slaves in early eighteenth century.

Hougan: a priest in the vodun (a.k.a. voodoo) neo-African religious cult of Haiti.

Kumina: a type of Myalism that stemmed from West African Ashanti ancestor possession beliefs; later incorporated Christian elements as a result of African-American influences in Jamaica, especially belief in possession by the Holy Spirit and baptism.

Loa: a deity of the Vodun cult in Haiti.

Myalism: strongest Neo-African cult in Jamaica, stemmed from ancient West African Ashanti ancestor possession cult and incorporates an African world-view understanding of nature, deity and human relationships.

Native Baptists: Afro-Jamaican (or Afro-Bahamian) Baptists who were influenced by orthodox Christian Afro-American Baptists from the British colonies (now United States) but incorporated aspects of African rituals and world-view into their preaching and worship. Native Baptists in Jamaica provided the leadership for slave revolts and Afro-Jamaican protests and confrontation by providing organizational resources and secure communities such as Black Churches in the United States did during the Civil Rights Movement. The Native Baptist leaders usually stressed church autonomy, the realization of freedom and the achievement of immediate political and economic opportunity for Afro-Jamaicans. The three Baptists preachers honored as Jamaican National Heroes were Native Baptists.

Particular Baptists: (a.k.a. Calvinist Baptist) believed in particular or restricted atonement, confined to the "elect" or those chosen by God to be saved. They also reject infant baptism and insisted on baptism by immersion. The British Missionary Society was the mission arm (subdivision) of the Particular Baptist Movement. Baptists who reject restricted atonement and believe that there is a general atonement (Jesus Christ died for all who believe and are baptized) are known as **General Baptists.** General Baptists were champions of religious toleration.

Pocomania: the union of Myalism and Protestant (especially Baptist) Christianity in Jamaica. This Neo-African religious movement promoted Christian Revivalism plus oral confessions, trances, dreams, prophecies, spirit seizures and frenzied dancing. It became the strongest of the native Jamaican religions until the emergence of Rastafarianism in the 1930's.

Rastafarianism (a.k.a. Raf Tafari): the name of an anti-white, back-to-Africa movement in Jamaica. The Rastas believe and teach that Emperor Haile Selassee of Ethiopia was the

Supreme Being and the only ruler of black people. Its phenomenal growth was based on its attraction of the more radical and displaced poor males of Jamaican society who needed a contemporary movement for protest and self-affirmation.

Revivalists: are known as Revival Zion, Zionist, Revival and Pocomania; a blend of Baptist, Methodist, Roman Catholic, Anglican, Pentecostal beliefs and practices with modified African beliefs and practices added.

Vodun (a.k.a. Voodoo): is a Neo-African syncretistic (blending) of religious rites and beliefs of a cult in Haiti. It is also a deity in the religion of the Aranda "nation" or tribe of Dahomey/Benin in West Africa.

Yoruba: a major tribe or ethnic group of southwestern Nigeria and eastern Dahomey/Benin.

BIBLIOGRAPHY

Alleyne, Mervyn C. *Roots of Jamaican Culture.* Kingston, University of West Indies Press, 1988.

Aristide, Jean-Bertrand. *Dignity.* Charlottesville, University Press of Virginia, 1966.

Barnes, Ian. *The Historical Atlas of the American Revolution.* New York, Rutledge, 2000.

Bethel Baptist Church, Nassau. *Bethel Baptist Church Bicentennial (1790-1990).* Nassau, August 5, 1990.

Bisnauth, Dale A. *A History of Religions in the Caribbean.* Kingston, Kingston Publishers, 1989.

Black Heritage Trail. *Boston African-American National Historic Site.* Boston, Museum of Afro-American History, Fall 2000.

Blassingame, John W. *The Slave Community: Plantation Life in the Antebellum South.* New York, Oxford Press, 1972.

Board of National Ministries. *Signs of Grace.* Valley Forge, American Baptist Churches, USA, Nov/Dec. 1988.

Brooks, Walter. "The Priority of the Silver Bluff Church," *Journal of Negro History*: Vol. VII, No. 32. Washington, D.C., Associated Press, April 1922.

____. *The Silver Bluff Church.* Washington, D.C., Press of R.L. Pendleton, 1910.

Brown, Beverly. *George Liele: Black Baptist and Pan Africanist, 1750-1826.* Savacou Vol. 11-12, September 1975.

Bryan, Patrick. *The Jamaican People, 1880-1902, Race, Class and Social Control.* Jamaica, The University of West Indies Press, 2000.

Burton, Richard D.E. *Afro-Creole: Power, Opposition, and Play in the Caribbean.* Ithaca, Cornell University Press, 1997.

Cattan, Louise Armstrong. *One Mark of Greatness: American Baptist Missions.* Philadelphia, Judson Press, 1961.

Cook, Richard B. *The Story of the Baptist in All Ages and Countries.* Greenfield, Mass., Wiley and Co., 1887.

Costen, Melva. *African American Christian Worship.* Nashville, Abington Press, 1993.

Courlander, Harold and Remy Bastien. *Religion and Politics In Haiti.* Washington, D.C.: Institute For Cross-Cultural Research, 1996.

Cratron, Michael. *Testing The Chains.* Ithaca: Cornell University Press, 1969.

Crum, Mason. *Gullah, Negro Life in the Carolina Sea Islands.* New York, Negro University Press, 1968.

Curtin, Philip. *The Atlantic Slave Trade: A Census.* Madison, University of Wisconsin Press, 1969.

_____. *Two Jamaicas: The Role of Idea in a Tropical Colony, 1830-1865.* Westport, CT., Greenwood Press, 1968.

Davis, Darien J. *Slavery and Beyond: The African Impact on Latin America and the Caribbean.* Wilimington, Wilmington Scholarly Resources, Inc., 1995

_____. "Kong in Haiti: A New Approach to Religious Syncretism" in *Slavery and Beyond,* by Luc de Heusch in *The African Impact on Latin America and the Caribbean.* Wilmington, Wilmington Scholarly Research, Inc., 1995

Dayan, Joan. *History and the Gods* Berkely/Los Angeles, University of California Press, 1999.

Dyfoot, Arthur Charles. *The Shaping Of The West Indian Church, 1492-1962.* Kingston, University of West Indies Press, 1999.

Erskine, Noel. *The Black Reformed Church.* New York, Reformed Church Press, 1978.

Estelle, Kenneth. *African American Worship.* Detroit, Visible Ink Press, 1944.

Felder, Cain Hope. *The Original African Heritage Study Bible (KJV).* Nashville, James C. Winston Publishing Company. 1993.

Fitts, Leroy. *The Lott Carey Legacy of African American Missions.* Baltimore, Gateway Press, 1993.

_____. *Lott Carey, First Black Missionary to Africa.* Valley Forge, Judson Press, 1978.

Franklin, John Hope. *From Slavery To Freedom,* Third Edition. New York, Alfred A. Knoph, 1967.

"Freedom To Be." *The Abolition of Slavery in Jamaica and its Aftermath,* Second Ed. Kingston, National Library of Jamaica.

Fulop, Timothy E. and Albert T. Raboteau. *African-American Religion: Interpretive Essays in History and Culture.* New York, Routledge, 1977.

Gayle, Clement. *George Liele, Pioneer Missionary To Jamaica.* Kingston, Jamaica Baptist Union, 1982.

Genovese, Eugene O. *Roll, Jordan, Roll.* New York, Vantage Books, 1976.

Graizer, S.D. *March in' The Pilgrims Home: Leadership Decision Making in an Afro-Caribbean Faith.* Westport, Connecticut, Greenwood Press, 1983.

Hamilton, Charles V. *The Black Preacher in America.* New York, William Morrow Company, 1972.

Heinl, Robert D. and Nancy G. *Written In Blood: The Study of the Haitian People.* Landham, Maryland, University Press of America, 1996.

Holmes, Edward A. *The Journal of Negro History.* Washington, D.C., Associated Press, 1966.

_____. "George Liele: Negro Slavery's Prophet of Deliverance" *The Baptist Quarterly,* October 1964. Philadelphia, Judson Press, 1964.

James, C.L.R. *The Black Jacobins.* New York, Random House, 1963.

Joel, Mirian. *African Traditions in Latin America.* Cuernavaca, Mexico, Centro Intercultural de Documentacion, No. 73, 1977.

Johnson, James Weldon. "Lift Every Voice And Sing," *National Baptist Hymnal.* Nashville, National Baptist Publishing Board, 1977.

Johnson, Howard. *The Bahamas in Slavery and Freedom.* Kingston, Ian Publishers Limited, 1991.

Jordan, Lewis G. "The Negro Preacher," *Baptist,* March 1928. Philadelphia, Judson Press.

Journal of Negro History I. "Letters Showing the Rise and Progress of Early Negro Churches in Georgia and West Indies." January 1916.

Landers, Jane. *Fort Mose, Gracia Real de Santa Teresa de Mose: A Free Black Town in Spanish Florida.* Gainesville, St. Augustine Historical Society, 1992.

Lawson, Winston Arthur. *Religion and Race: African and European Roots In Conflict—A Jamaican Testament.* New York, Peter Lang Publishing, Inc., 1996.

Leburn, James, G. *The Haitian People.* New Haven: Yale University Press, 1941.

"Letters Showing the Rise and Progress of Early Negro Churches in Georgia and West Indies," *Journal of Negro History, I (January 1916)*

Lewis, Gordon K. *The Growth of the Modern West Indies.* New York, Monthly Review Press, 1968.

Martin, Sandy Dwayne. *Black Baptist and African Missions: The Origin of a Movement (1830-1915).* Macon, Georgia, Mercer, 1989.

Massachusetts Baptist Missionary Society. *The Minutes of the Massachusetts Baptist Missionary Society (March 5).* Cambridge, 1823.

Merriam, Edmund Franklin. *History of American Baptist Missions.* Philadelphia, American Baptist Publication Society, 1913.

Metrauix, Alfred. *Voodoo In Haiti.* Brooklyn, Schocken Books, Inc., 1972

Nagashima, Yoshiko S. *Rastafarian Music in Contemporary Jamaica.* Tokyo, Institute for the Study of Languages and Cultures in Asia and Africa, 1984.

Oliver, John and Lois E. Horton. *Black Bostonians* New York, Holmes and Meler Publisher, Inc., Revised Edition, 1979.

Ottley, A. Roy and William J. Weatherby. *The Negro In New York* Dobbs Ferry, Oceana Publications, Inc., 1967.

Pageant Book (1735-1935) Augusta Bicentennial Augusta, Georgia, 1935.

Pamphile, Leon D. *Haitians and African Americans (A Heritage of Tragedy and Hope)* Gainesville, University Press of Florida, 2001.

Phillippo Baptist Church *175th Anniversary Booklet, 1818-1993* Spanish Town, W. Alwyn Sutherland and Co. LTD, 1993.

Powell, C., Editor *Bethel Willing Workers Newsletter, Vol. 3.* Nassau, Bethel Baptist Church, 2002.

Pressoir, Docteur C. *Le Protestantisme Haitien, Second Vol.* Haiti, Imprimerie du Seminaire Adventiste, 1976.

Pryne, Earnest A. *Freedom In Jamaica.* London, The Carey Press, 1833.

Pugh, Alfred L. *African Religions in the West Indies and the United States* (an unpublished Manuscript) Lauderhill, Florida, 1997.

Raboteau, Albert J. *Slave Religion.* Oxford, Oxford University Press, 1980.

Riley, Sandra. *Homeward Bound.* Miami, Island Research, 1983.

Rippon, John. "Account of the Life of Mr. David George." *The Baptist Annual Register.* London, 1790-1793

Romain, Charles Poisset. *Le Protestantisme Dans La Society Haitienne.* Haiti Imprimene. Henri Deschamps, 1986.

Russell, Horace O. *The Missionary Outreach of the West Indian Church in the Nineteenth Century.* New York, P. Lang, 2000.

Russell-Backford, Sybil. *Bahamas Baptist Union; Glimpses of the First Ninety Years (1892-1982).* Nassau, Bahamas Baptist Union, 1982.

Sheller-Mimi. *Democracy After Slavery.* Gainesville, University Press of Florida, 2000.

Sherlock, Phillip and Hazel Bennett. *The Story of the Jamaican People.* Kingston, Ian Randle Publishers, 1998.

Shurden, Walter B. *The Baptist Identity: Four Fragile Freedoms.* Macon, Smyth and Helwys Publishing, Inc., 1995.

Simpson, George Eaton. *Black Religion in the New World.* New York, Columbia University Press, 1978.

Sowell, Thomas. *Ethnic America (A History).* New York: Basic Books, Inc., 1981.

Stanley, Brian. *The History Of The Baptist Missionary Society (1792-1992).* Edinburgh, T & T Clark, 1992.

Sunshine, Catherine A. *The Caribbean: Survival, Struggle and Sovereignty.* Washington, D.C., Ecumenical Program of Central America and the Caribbean, 1973.

Symonette, Michael C. and Antonia Canzoneri. *Baptists in the Bahamas.* El Paso, Baptist Spanish Publication House, 1979.

Symonetti, The Rev. Michael C. *A Personal Interview in Nassau, New Providence, Bahama Islands* January 7, 2000.

Tannenbaum, Frank. "The Destiny of the Negro in the Western Hamisphere." *Political Science Quarterly*, March 1946.

Turner, Mary. *Slaves and Missionaries,* Urbana/Chicago, University of Illinois Press, 1982.

Tyson, George F. *Toussaint L'Ouverture.* Englewood Cliffs, Prentice Hall, Inc., 1967.

Underhill, E.B. *The Life of James Murcell Phillippo.* London, Jackson, Wolford and Hodden, 1881.

Waddell, D.A.G. *The West Indies and the Guianas.* Englewood Cliffs, Prentice Hall, Inc., 1967.

Wagner, Clarence M. *Profiles of Black Georgia Baptists.* Atlanta, Bennett Brothers Publishing Co. 1980.

Walker, Williston. *A History of the Christian Church.* New York, Charles Scribner's Sons, 1970.

White, P. Anthony. *The Baptist Came and the Bahamas Was Never the Same.* Nassau, Punch Publications, Ltd., Friday, October 16, 1998.

Williams, Eric. *From Columbus to Castro: The History of the Caribbean, 1492-1969.* New York, Harper and Ross, 1970.

Wilmore, Gayraud S. *Black Religion and Black Radicalism.* Garden City, Doubleday and Company, *1972*

Woodson, Carter G. *The History Of The Negro Church.* Washington, The Associated Publishers, 1972.

World Almanac 2000.